P9-DHC-981

*Heidegger Memorial Lectures*

# Heidegger Memorial Lectures

*Edited by* / Werner Marx

*Translated by* / Steven W. Davis

WITHDRAWN

DUQUESNE UNIVERSITY PRESS

Theodore Lownik Library
Illinois Benedictine College
Lisle, Illinois 60532

B
3279
•H49
G24513
1982

First published in German as *Heidegger: Freiburger Universitätsvortväge Zu Seinem Gedenken*

© H.-G Gadamer, W. Marx, C. F. v. Weizsäcker, 1977

English translation Copyright © 1982 by Duquesne University Press

Published by Duquesne University Press
600 Forbes Avenue
Pittsburgh, PA 15282

All Rights reserved.
Printed in the United States of America. No part of this book may be used or reproduced in any manner whatsoever without written permission except in the case of brief quotations for use in critical articles and reviews.

*Library of Congress Cataloging in Publication Data.*

Gadamer, Hans Georg, 1900–
  Heidegger memorial lectures.

  Translation of: Heidegger, Freiburger Universitätsvortväge zu seinem Gedenken / H.-G. Gadamer, W. Marx, C.F. von Weizsäcker.
  Contents: Introduction / Helmut Engler—Thinking and its matter / Werner Marx—Being, spirit, God / Hans-Georg Gadamer—Heidegger and natural science / Carl Friedrich von Weizsäcker.
  1. Heidegger, Martin, 1889–1976—Addresses, essays, lectures. I. Marx, Werner.  II. Davis, Steven W.  III. Weizsäcker, Carl Friedrich, Freiherr von, 1912–  IV. Title.
  B3279.H49G24513          193          82–5112
  ISBN 0–8207–0154–8                   AACR2

# Contents

# Key to Abbreviations

**German Texts**

Hw      *Holzwege*. Frankfurt a. M.: Vittorio Klostermann, 1950.

VA      *Vorträge und Aufsätze*. Pfullingen: Verlag Günther Neske, 1954.

UzS      *Unterwegs zur Sprache*. Pfullingen: Verlag Günther Neske, 1959.

WdW      *Vom Wesen der Wahrheit*. Frankfurt a. M.: Vittorio Klostermann, 1967.

PLW      *Platons Lehre von der Wahrheit*. Bern: A. Francke Verlag, 1947.

SvG      *Der Satz vom Grund*. Pfullingen: Verlag Günther Neske, 1957.

WhD      *Was heisst Denken?* Tübingen: Max Niemeyer Verlag, 1954.

ZSD    *Zur Sache des Denkens*. Tübingen: Max Miemerer Verlag, 1969.

ZW    "Die Zeit des Weltbildes," in Hw (p. 69-104).

FT    "Die Frage nach der Technik," in VA (pp. 13-44).

WB    *"Wissenschaft und Besinnung,"* in VA (pp. 45-70).

SZ    *Sein und Zeit*. 12th ed. Tübingen: Max Niemeyer Verlag, 1972.

DS    *Die Kategorien-und Bedentungslehre des Duns Scotus*. Tübingen: J.C.B. Mohr, 1916.

**English Texts**

OTB    *On Time and Being* (Translated by Joan Stambaugh. New York: Harper and Row, 1972 (*Zur Sache des Denkens*).

WCT    *What Is Called Thinking?* Translated by J. Glenn Gray and Fred Wieck. New York: Harper and Row, 1968 (*Was heisst Denken?*)

BT    *Being and Time*. Translated by John Macquarrie and Edward Robinson. Oxford: Basil Blackwell, 1962 (*Sein und Zeit*).

WL    *On the Way to Language*. Translated by Peter D. Hertz. New York: Harper and Row, 1971 (*Unterwegs zur*

*Sprache,* except for "Die Sprache" [pp. 9-34], which appears in translation in PLT).

PLT     *Poetry, Language, Thought.* Translated by Albert Hofstadter. New York: Harper and Row, 1971 (in addition to "Die Sprache" contains selected texts from *Holzwege* and *Vorträge und Aufsätze*).

BW     *Martin Heidegger: Basic Writings.* Edited by David Farrell Krell. New York: Harper and Row, 1977 (selected texts ranging chronologically from *Sein und Zeit* to *Zur Sache des Denkens*.)

QT     *The Question Concerning Technology and Other Essays.* Translated by William Lovitt. New York: Harper and Row, 1977 ("Die Frage nach der Technik," "Die Zeit des Weltbildes," and "Wissenschaft und Besinnung").

# Translator's Preface

*". . . for every translation is in itself already an interpretation."* [1]

The German edition of this book contains the following remarks:

> This book contains three lectures that were delivered in connection with the University of Freiburg's commemoration of Martin Heidegger on December 16, 1976. Werner Marx spoke on "Thinking and Its Matter," Hans-Georg Gadamer on "Being, Spirit, God," and Carl-Friedrich von Weizsäcker on "Heidegger and Natural Science."
>
> Werner Marx's lecture interprets the entire Heideggerian enterprise from the standpoint of the late writings by asking:
>
> 1. How did Heidegger define metaphysical thinking?
> 2. To what extent or in what way was his thinking already transformed, that is, different from metaphysical thinking?
> 3. Wherein did he see the matter of transformed thinking?
>
> The discussion of these questions shows how Heidegger defined anew the essence of time and truth and thereby came to

---

1. Martin Heidegger, *Heraklit*: . *Der Anfang der Abendlandlischen Denkens*; 2. *Logik. Heraklits Lehre vom Logos, Gesamtausgabe* (Frankfurt a M.: Vittorio Klostermann, 1977), p. 63.

conceive preparatorily other fundamental determinations of the occurrence of Being. With their help he sketched the picture of a structure within which man could dwell and which would save him from the highest danger that prevails in the age of technology.

Heidegger's reawakening of the question of Being is developed in several respects in Hans-Georg Gadamer's lecture: (a) in view of the religious problematic of talking about God, (b) in delimitation from the classical metaphysics of Aristotle and Hegel, and (c) positively in experiences that have become inaccessible as a result of modern subjective thought and the challenge to humanity that the essence of modern technology constitutes.

Carl Friedrich von Weizsäcker's lecture continues the dialogue between Heidegger and natural science. First of all, Heidegger's definitions of the essence of natural science and technology in his late writings are presented. Then, by going back to the newly published early writings, the relation of logic, ontology, and natural science is clarified. Finally, Professor Weizsäcker formulates the response of a physicist— with this conclusion: Up to now natural science has not understood what Heidegger had to say to it, and conversely Heidegger was not able to think natural science thoroughly down to its foundation.

These notes state very succinctly what is to be found in each of the lectures contained in this book. There is no need to repeat what is said so well here. Furthermore, little commentary on the lectures is called for because they themselves bring out the leading issues in Heidegger. Indeed any attempt to bring out the highlights of their lectures would be at best a repetition of what is already contained in them in a concise way.

Consequently I would like to make only one observation with regard to the subject matter of the lectures—one that

may not be readily apparent from what is said above—
namely, that which the lectures have in common, which is
precisely the guiding theme throughout Heidegger's thinking. This also leads to some comments that should be made
about this translation.

The matter that occupied Heidegger's thinking throughout
his life was the question of the meaning of Being. This point
is brought out particularly in the two lectures by Professor Marx and Gadamer. This matter, however, underwent
changes—more properly, transformations—which are discussed in all three lectures but especially in those of Professors Gadamer and Weizsäcker. This transformation manifested itself in a change in Heidegger's language, wherein
Being was not always the explicit matter under discussion.
But this very change in the language used to "describe" the
matter being pursued also points to the difficulty that
Heidegger had in finding the proper language to discuss what
he was pursuing in his thinking (compare Professor
Gadamer's lecture on this point). Of course the situation was
not as simple as this; that is to say, it was not a simple case of
having a subject matter and then finding the proper language
to describe it, as if it were simply there waiting to be named
(compare Professor Marx's lecture on this point). Thinking
itself was transformed, and this means—given the relationship between thinking and the matter at issue for it (again, see
Professor Marx's lecture)—that the matter also changed or,
more precisely, was itself transformed. This is one reason
why Heidegger's language changed. But it was not merely
his terminology that changed; his concept of the essence of
language also underwent development. Consequently one
must keep an eye not only on Being but also an the terms used

13

to discuss it and the way language itself is used. In other words, the matter most at issue in these three lectures—as in Heidegger's own thought—is Being and the speaking and thinking of it. What is Being and how may it be approached—or how does it approach us—in thinking and speaking? This is what is at stake in Heidegger's thought, and it is this theme—in its various manifestations and connections with other issues central to it (for example, *physis, logos, aletheia*) and on its periphery—that appears in the lectures of this book, lectures that attempt to practice in varying degrees a "recollective preparatory thinking."

The discussion of Being and language brings us to some comments about the present translation. This translation is not at all times a literal translation in the sense of being a "scientifically" exact translation simply because this is not possible with Heidegger (the third section of Professor Weizsäcker's lecture shows why this is so). It is not possible because he plays on the meaning of words and also because his language undergoes the development mentioned above, so that a term that means one thing at one point in the course of his thought can come to be used in a different way or take on an importance that it did not previously have and thereby undergo a change in emphasis or meaning (for example, *die Lichtung*, not to mention *das Ereignis*; compare Professor Marx's lecture). This can be noted in the Glossary below where some key terms have more than one meaning. It is also necessary to have this leeway in translating the present text because it contains lectures by three different men and, although they may use approximately the same terminology to develop their themes, they may also take them from different periods in Heidegger's thought, which makes flexibility necessary for the reason stated above.

However, there is an even more important philosophical reason why a translation of Heidegger—or of works on him that focus on the path of his thinking and its matter—cannot be "scientifically literal." To demand a static or fixed literalness of translation would be to fall into one of the traps mentioned by Professor Gadamer toward the end of his lecture, namely, the congealing of language so that it loses its flexibility. The demand for literalness is the demand for scientificality, objectivity, and certainty—in this case, in language—which is simply subscribing to the dominant conception of truth of modernity and applying it to the "use" of language. This demand has a limited place in the realm of thinking and what is to be thought, if it has a place at all.

Having said all the above, however, it should be mentioned, if it need be, that the translation is not arbitrary by any stretch of the imagination; it merely attempts to follow the matter at issue in the text and in the thought of Heidegger. This of course has its own specific difficulty. To cite a point made toward the end of Professor Marx's lecture in a slightly different but still relevant way: What is the "standard" for the hearing, and consequently the translating, of that which is said in these lectures? But, just as Professor Marx does in his lecture, we must leave that question explicitly unanswered here. In fact, it is that question that drives us back to the lectures and to Heidegger's thought and the matter at issue, because only by going to them can such a "standard" manifest itself.

Although I have taken into account the English translations of Heidegger's texts, the translations from his works are my own. However, I have followed as closely as possible the conventions of the translation of key Heideggerian terms so that this text can be easily related to extant English translations of Heidegger's works.

With regard to the citations of Heidegger's texts, two things need to be noted. First, in the present translation the first abbreviation within the parentheses after a quote refers to the German edition of the text; the second abbreviation, to the English edition. Second, the list of the texts in the "Key to Abbreviations" (at the front of the book) includes only those texts referred to in the present set of lectures. Furthermore, the English texts cited refer only to those books or essays that were referred to in the German edition of this book; thus for example, *Poetry, Language, Thought* and *The Question Concerning Technology and Other Essays,* not to mention *Martin Heidegger: Basic Writings,* contain texts other than those noted in the remarks after their entry in the list; but since they were not cited in the present book they have not been included in the remarks.

Finally I would like to acknowledge the help of these people at various stages of the translation: Reginald Lilly, who went over the entire manuscript and made many helpful suggestions, Professor Werner Marx, who provided helpful comments on his lecture, and Professor John Sallis.

AM INSELWALL
*Braunschweig*

# Foreword

Heidegger's demand was to carry forward his thought in such a way that others would be able to take up his questioning at the point to which he had brought it. For that reason, Albert-Ludwigs-Universität Freiburg i. Br. remembered Heidegger not by the customary academic *laudatio,* but rather by these lectures—delivered on December 16, 1976, in the *Auditorium Maximum*—that brought his work into view by considering crucial aspects of it. This is also the purpose of this publication on the first anniversary of his death, May 26, 1977.

# Introduction

*by Helmut Engler, Rector*

My very esteemed ladies and gentlemen, in the name of Albert-Ludwigs-Universtät and its four philosophical faculties I cordially welcome you to this set of lectures. On May 26, 1976, Martin Heidegger died. The Philosophical Seminar I, the four faculties of the old Freiburg Philosophical Faculty, and the University to which Martin Heidegger had belonged as Emeritus University Professor have invited you to these proceedings, which are dedicated to the memory of this great thinker.

The external setting of our academic meeting is modest and simple. Unpretentiousness in outward appearance corresponds to the manner of the man whose memory is to be honored. It also appears to be appropriate for the relation that existed between Martin Heidegger and his university for the last few decades. That this relation did not conform to the norm is no secret, and it can be only surprising that great minds had difficulties in rectifying the situation. This is certainly not the right place for the present rector of Albert-Ludwigs-Universität to discuss these difficulties, which were painful not only for Martin Heidegger but also for many members of the university. I believe, however, that I should not suppress the fact that during Heidegger's lifetime we did not succeed entirely in dealing with the past. It would be dishonest if we simply passed over this fact; we could be reproached for being presumptuous and expressing a careless attitude if, without acknowledging our awareness that a residue of the past remained unmastered and always would, we included Martin Heidegger as one of our own today and expected that a reflection of his importance would fall upon this university.

Albert-Ludwigs-Universität will preserve an enduring memory of Martin Heidegger as *its* professor, as the great philosopher and teacher. It will also preserve a memory of him as the man who accomplished his great life's work here, who lived in its spacious passageways, and whose world-encompassing spirit was fully at one with his embrace of his Messkirch home and simple life in the Black Forest.

I must thank you very much, esteemed ladies and gentlemen, for being present here today and taking part in this memorial event. Many of you have come a long way in order to be here; many, who have admired Martin Heidegger as their great Freiburg and fellow Baden countryman, have come from the city or surrounding areas. Of the great number of guests, I would like to name only Professor André Mercier, who is the General Secretary of the Fédération Internationale des Sociétés de Philosophie and representative of the world philosophical community. However, I would also like to note the presence of the representatives of the resident philosophical societies in Germany and abroad, the numerous university teachers of philosophy and the other sciences who are assembled here, and the honorable senators of our university. In addition, I would like to sincerely welcome the representatives of the younger groups of our university—

scientific assistants and students—who are present in large numbers. And I gratefully observe that Dr. Hermann Heidegger, Mr. Jörg Heidegger, and other relatives of the family have come to this event.

Finally, I bid an especially sincere welcome to the gentlemen whose lectures we will attend immediately following this and later this afternoon. Professor Marx is due our special gratitude for the fact that he has undertaken the opening lecture and, moreover, has borne the weight of the greatest part of the preparation for this event. It is a great honor for the university and its philosophical faculties that Professors Hans-Georg Gadamer and Carl Friedrich von Weizsäcker have accepted our invitation and will speak to us this afternoon. Because of their presence, this memorial event for Martin Heidegger becomes a high point in our academic life, one that stands above the everyday events of the university. For this reason I express a particularly sincere thanks to both speakers for not having refused our request, and I believe that in doing so I express the sentiment of all who are present here.

# Thinking and its Matter

*by Werner Marx*

In the Preface to a collection of texts that were reissued under the title *Wegmarken* in the year 1967, Heidegger said:

> He who sets out on the path of thinking knows least about that which as the determining matter—from behind and beyond him as it were—moves him toward it.

This acknowledgment by Martin Heidegger attests to the fact that he in no way considered thinking as his property. As a result he shared this conviction with many philosophers. For example, for Hegel, in contrast to the concept of thinking as a "subjective activity," thinking was the "active universal." I said "as a result" because the experience that led Heidegger to the conviction that the nature of thinking is nonsubjective was an entirely different one.

Heidegger also shared with others the view that that which is thought, the "work," has a Being fully independent from the person of the thinker: in a work the truth of the matter itself comes to the fore.

Thus it would run counter to Heidegger's fundamental convictions if we were to remember him today in a biographical way.[1] We must rather devote ourselves to his

---

1. I thank the Rector for having already named an additional reason for not proceeding in this fashion.

thought and his work. But what does "work" mean to Heidegger? *This* work, of course, is not a closed and complete whole; it is not a system. For Heidegger philosophizing was possible only as questioning that always begins anew. It would be a mistake, therefore, to treat his questions as if they were results that could be collected together in a synopsis. Yet all of these questions had this in common: all were ways of *thinking*; all were concerned with *one* matter, *one* task of thinking. To be sure, in contrast to tradition they were ways of transformed thinking and transformed matter. If we consider that for Heidegger nothing less depends on the transformation of thinking and its matter than preparation for the arrival of "the saving" [*das Rettende*] within the prevailing "highest danger" for mankind today, then we must ask, What did Heidegger in fact mean by thinking, and what did he consider as its present and future matter and task? These questions underlie Heidegger's entire endeavor.

According to academic custom the task falls to me to portray as a whole the work of the deceased. The thoughts of such an extremely complicated thinker as Heidegger cannot be reproduced simply; any such portrayal must be the result of long years of interpretation. This holds true to a high degree for his later writings. However, it is from these works that I would like to take up these questions because up to now the research on Heidegger has not interpreted these texts so that one might see how Heidegger's entire concern follows from them. The attempt to show this is my contribution to this event, which should remember Heidegger but not in the customary form of a *laudatio*. By means of interpreting his later writings—largely reserving my own views—I hope to comply with Heidegger's demand to pass his thought on in such a way that others are able to take up his questioning at precisely the point to which he brought it.

In this sense I regard his last publication as his legacy. It bears the title, "The End of Philosophy and the Task of Thinking" (ZSD 61 ff. : OTB 55 ff.; also BW 373 ff.). The first sentences of this text read:

> The title names the attempt of a reflection that persists in questioning. Questions are pathways to an answer. If the answer were once to become granted, it would consist of a transformation of thinking, not of an assertion about a state of affairs [ZSD 61 : OTB 55, BW 373].

On the matter of the "task of thinking," he says:

> When we ask about the task of thinking, this means, within the horizon of philosophy, to determine that which concerns thinking, that which for thinking is still in dispute, that which is the matter in dispute. In the German language the word *Sache* signifies this [ZSD 67 : OTB 61, BW 379].

To clarify the two questions, What did Heidegger consider as thinking? and What did he consider as its matter? we pose in this lecture the following three principal questions: (a) How did Heidegger define thinking as it existed previously, that is, the thinking of metaphysics? (b) In what way was Heidegger's own thinking already transformed, already "different" from that which existed previously? and (c) Wherein did he see the task, the matter, of "transformed thinking?"

These questions stand in a relationship that intrinsically prohibits an isolated treatment of them one after another. The answer to the first question may depend upon the answer to the second: presumably only transformed thinking would be able to define the thinking that existed prior to it. Then too, can the essence of transformed thinking be determined without an answer to the third question, that is, the question about the task and the matter? We like to think that there is no thinking without a matter. In thinking, which "persists in questioning" in the sense of the paragraph quoted above, however, there takes place a reciprocal action, that is, a mutual self-altering of thinking and matter. Yet this does not appear to be Heidegger's view because for him the matter is "that which is to be thought." And it has the character of a "call," which sends us questioningly upon the way (WhD 103 ff. : WCT 165). Accordingly, questioning would have only this ancillary function: to "correspond or conform to" the matter, the task. If we followed this view of the relation of matter and thinking, we would have to speak first of the *matter* of thinking. Concerning the matter of thinking, however, Heidegger declares in this essay that it "has closed itself off from philosophy," and this means from metaphysics —which begins with Plato and Aristotle—and I quote, "In its beginning, even by means of its beginning" (ZSD 66 : OTB 59). It is the hitherto "unthought" of metaphysics.

Thus we come back to the first question—the question of how Heidegger defined the thinking of metaphysics. Heidegger sought to show in numerous texts that it had the character of "rational representational thought." But in what way was it representational thought? Did "reason" actually take place as a representational thought in the different determinations in which the tradition conceived it? Heidegger, of course, does not wish to present this in terms of its changing conceptions in the history of thinking (cp. WhD 27 f. : WCT 60 ff.); rather he wishes to determine the *essence* of reason but only insofar as it occurred as *ratio*. In the rationality of the *animal rationale*—that is, its capacity to perceive what is, what can be, and what ought to be—he recognizes a manifold "placing" [*Stellen*], and he is concerned to show that this placing has developed in modern thought into a placing-before-oneself [*Vor-sich-stellen*]. With the *ego cogito* of Descartes it emerges as the kind of Being of the subject.

His *cogitatio* as *repräsentatio* takes place as a placing-before-oneself of something from oneself, whereby what is thus placed-before-oneself becomes the object, which is at the disposal of and is masterable by calculative thought [*das Berechnen*]. This interpretation of modern philosophy has certainly not gone undisputed. Indeed the Cartesian *cogitatio* was not only a placing of the object before oneself, and accordingly a relating of the object back to the representing subject, but also a simultaneous relating of that which is given to its origin in God. Similar objections on the further development of the concept of representation can be formulated from the works of Spinoza, Kant, Fichte, and Hegel.

However, we are not concerned here with a critique of the Heideggerian interpretation of the philosophical tradition; rather, we ask further, What does Heidegger mean when he speaks of rational representational thought? Representational thought is defined by a claim to furnish rational grounds [*Gründen*], a claim that has ruled all thought since the Greeks (cp. SvG 54). For the Greeks that which is [*das was ist*] could be thought of only with regard to its rational character as "being." And thus, according to Heidegger, the Being of that which is, of beings, is considered self-evidently and unquestioningly by all metaphysics as the ground (*ratio*). Being as ground (*ratio*) has appeared in metaphysics in many different forms: as the transcendental condition of the objectivity of objects, as the dialectical mediation of the movement of absolute spirit, and even as the historical process of production. Heidegger's view, to be sure, does not take into consideration the great differences that lie in the specific determination of the rational grounding relation [*Begründungszusammenhanges*] in the individual positions in metaphysics, for instance, in Kant, Fichte, and Hegel. However, in seeking an answer to just this question it is important that for Heidegger, as a consequence of Being considered as ground (*ratio*), the *matter* in metaphysical thought lay only in the grounding of and the giving of reasons for beings. According then to the above passage, "since its beginning and *by means of* its beginning," they have obstructed the view of *the* matter which was, for Heidegger's entire lifetime, that which is to be thought: Being itself. For him this "forgetfulness" of Being is the necessary result of the history of Western thought conceived in a definite way, and it is precisely on that account that "hitherto existing thought"—that is, metaphysical thought—remains throughout rational representational thought.

With that we leave our first question and turn now to the second: In what way was Heidegger's own thinking already transformed, different compared to metaphysical thinking?

Was Heidegger's thinking actually something so radically new? Did he not merely develop further the phenomenology of Husserl, who after all understood himself as one carrying forward European philosophy and who above all wished to bring to completion the beginnings of Descartes and transcendental philosophy in his transcendental phenomenology?

In fact Heidegger himself declared more than once that he

understood his own thinking as phenomenological. In a 1969 publication he made it known that phenomenology is "self-transforming and because of this an enduring possibility of thinking" (ZSD 90 : OTB 82). It has been much disputed how far Heidegger, Husserl's assistant, remained faithful to phenomenology. *Being and Time* is considered by many to be phenomenological, while Heidegger's later thought is not. However, one must ask what Heidegger in *Being and Time* understood by "phenomenon" and *logos*. We know from his own recollection that even before *Being and Time* he had in his encounter with Aristotle come to a completely new interpretation of the fundamental concepts of phenomenon—*logos*—and, more importantly truth, which the Greeks had called *aletheia*. According to Heidegger, the Greek word *aletheia* can be suitably characterized only through the meaning that lies in the German word *Un-verborgenheit* [unconcealment]. Accordingly, he understood the related verb *aletheuein* as *Entbergen* [uncovering]. He said in *Being and Time* that truth must "always first be wrested from beings"; beings must be "torn from concealment" (SZ 222 : BT 265). His other two fundamental concepts also followed from this meaning of truth. Thus he translates *logos* as *offenbarmachen* [to make manifest, open] and *phainesthai* as *sich zeigen* [self-showing]. This new interpretation of the fundamental Greek concepts was, according to information from Heidegger himself, the preparation for his understanding of phenomenology—of course, together with the experience of the phenomenological ideas that he gained from discussions with Husserl. Nevertheless, from the moment that Husserl's phenomenology conceived itself as a transcendental method that analyzes the intentional acts of human consciousness,

Heidegger distanced himself from it. What links him with Husserl, even in his last works, is the motto "To the things [*Sachen*] themselves," the viewing of the "phenomena." But this "viewing" was not, as it was for Husserl, intuiting oriented toward the perception of things, intuiting that Husserl held as the "principle of all principles." It was a readiness for experience that just cannot be characterized with the help of traditional definitions. Heidegger attempted to elucidate it with ever new turns of expression. Thus he once spoke, strangely enough, of a "visual leap" [*Blicksprung*] (WhD 141 : WCT 233) in order to clarify that in no way in the beholding [*Erblicken*] of a phenomenon does the matter to be thought "stand over against" the thinking of it, as in the representing of an object; on the contrary, it has the character of an element to which one gives oneself over, into which one "leaps." However, more important still, this readiness for experience is considered by him as the "simplicity of being able to hear" (UzS 207: WL 101; cp. SvG 86). In his reflection upon the "essence of language" he defined this hearing as the hearing of the silent address [*Zusage*] of that which is there for thinking to think (UzS 179 : WL 75), and as such he called it the "gesture of thinking" that precedes questioning, because questioning about [*Nachfragen*] is borne by the address that which is to come into question (UzS 180 : WL 75).

In any case, there is no doubt that Heidegger's "method" of philosophizing changed early on. It was a "hermeneutic of the facticity of *Dasein*" even before *Being and Time*. He had already departed, in *Being and Time*, from the fundamental ontological definitions of metaphysics with his "destruction" of the history of ontology—especially its categories of substantiality and subjectivity—as well as with his analytic of the constitution of the Being of that existing being that understands Being [*die Analytik der Seinsverfassung der seinsverstehenden Existenz*]. However, it was two years after *Being and Time* that he first gained the freedom to ask the fundamental question: What is metaphysics?

Forty-seven years ago—at this point, this biographical remark is permissible—Heidegger discussed this question in his Freiburg inaugural lecture. I myself attended the lecture, and I still remember how his answer provoked the scholars of the university. In retrospect I believe that only a way of thinking that had already moved outside of metaphysics could have taken Kant's doctrine of the anchoring of metaphysics in the "nature of man" as the point of departure for the concept that metaphysical thinking has its origin in the fundamental constitution of man, that is, transcendence, on the basis of which he is always *metà-tà physikà*, beyond the whole of beings, and has transcended it as a whole. Only a way of thinking that had already freed itself from the ontological concepts of metaphysics could have interpreted this fundamental movement as a surmounting that leads not to the highest "being,"—to God, Who grounds the essence of man and nonhuman beings in His Being—but a surmounting that leads into a sphere that is precisely not a being but rather the radical Other in comparison with beings—the Nothing [*das Nichts*]—and only this way of thinking could have seen in this being immersed in the Nothing the ontological meaning of *Dasein*, which encounters itself precisely not in the manner of an absolute rational self-grounding but in the finitude of its historical facticity. Only thinking that had already dissociated itself from the rational thinking of philosophy could attempt to make visible the power of the Nothing in the experience of anxiety, that mood over which man has no control. It is through this insight into the powerlessness inherent in man that Heidegger left behind the rational representational thought of metaphysics. It is in this insight that the "turning" of his thought prepared itself—an insight for which the power of the Nothing consisted in making manifest the Being of beings.

The quintessence of Heidegger's "turning" lies in his experience that that which is thought is not the result of an accomplishment of subjectivity, that is, of a rational or transcendental constituting thought, but rather that that which is thought presented itself [*sich zudachte*] to him or, more precisely, announced [*zusprach*] itself to him. Incumbent in Heidegger's understanding of himself in this way was his view that his thinking was "needed" by the matter, which—in Heidegger's words, quoted at the outset—"moves" the one who thinks "from behind and beyond him—moves him toward it." Thinking that is thus "turned" may call to mind traditions of Western thinking such as we find in Neoplatonism, mysticism and in the middle period of Schelling. Their matter, however, was God and the occurrence of His revelation. But what is the matter of Heideggerian thought? Thus we come to our third and most important principal question.

However, before I interpret Heidegger's concept of the "matter of thinking," I would like to interrupt my presentation and note that I myself am convinced that, in view of the present predominance of functionalistic ways of thinking, it is the matter, the task, of thinking to pose the question concerning the determination of the essence of essence [*des Wesens des Wesens*]. This has nothing to do with so-called essentialism. The discrediting of the question of essence as "essentialistic" in certain varieties of the new positivism proceeds from the tacit assumption that essence can be thought of only as substance. In consequence of its origin from the Aristotelian *ousia*, essence thought as substance is concerned with the form and content of beings, whose independence is guaranteed by means of universality. If it is a question of the determination of the essence of beings, I leave open for now how the essence of essence would be thought differently. In any case, where it is a question of the determination of the shape of reality as a whole—the essence of Being conceived in this way—I see the task as one of thinking essence in a way that corresponds to this matter.

In Aristotelian tradition man was unable to intervene in the prevailing essential order of beings in a way that would alter it. Because of the successes of the experimental natural sciences and the insights of the humanities, this view—with regard to beings—has largely lost acceptance. Concerning this, our historical consciousness further requires that a transformation of reality as a whole, the dawning of a "new period," be thinkable in such a way that man has a role in this transformation. The essence of essence, which refers to the whole, would be thought of not as "eternal" but in such a way that it—as that which prevails at any given time—would have determined its epoch, and the participation of man in this would be thought of in such a way that the danger of a historicizing, relativizing, and "anthropomorphizing" of essence would be excluded.

Because of the transcendental turn and Hegel's insights in the *Phenomenology of Spirit*, the new philosophy had already made thinkable the possibility of the "birth of and transition to a new period" (Hamburg, 1956, p. 15) as well as the essence of man as an agent who alters reality. However, on the categorical level Hegel quite plainly excluded the possibility of the advent of an entirely new "spirit," because, even if for him subjectivity—as the power of negativity— were able to dissolve the congealedness of substance, never- theless the absolute knowing that knows itself must think of itself from the vantage point of the identity of absolute sub- jectivity and objectivity, and thus it remains bound to the system of thinking-determinations and thought-determina- tions which, since as a system it is complete in itself, can never be supplemented by a new category.

How then can Heidegger see the matter of thinking? By now this much is clear: for Heidegger the matter was not a fixed content but rather the task of thinking—of present as well as of future thinking. In his determination of the matter Heidegger traveled many paths, the direction of which changed often, although, as stated above, they all always remained directed toward *one* matter.

We shall attempt to determine these directions and to dis- cuss a few "stations" along that path. Indeed the character of this thinking as a pathway excludes an all-embracing defini- tion of the "task of thinking in Heidegger."

The declared matter of thinking in *Being and Time* was the question concerning "the meaning of the Being of beings" (cp. SZ §2). To be sure, the theme of the published part was only the kind of Being of that being to whom the understand- ing of Being essentially belongs—*Dasein*. In the analytic of *Dasein* the meaning of this understanding of Being lay in a horizon that Heidegger, in a new manifest understanding of time, defined as a temporal horizon. To understand how the later Heidegger again took up the question concerning the meaning of Being, which was not dealt with in *Being and Time*, one must take into consideration the fact that from that point forward he defined Being in terms of time. This holds true as well for the different ways in which—as we discussed—the rational representational thought of metaphysics conceived Being as ground, just as it also holds true for the matter of "transformed thinking." By means of the interpretation of decisive texts on metaphysics, Heidegger attempted above all to show that in the Being represented explicitly or implicitly by metaphysics the temporal meaning of presence [*Gegenwart*] was also always represented.

For Heidegger this temporal meaning of Being—that is, Being as presence [*Gegenwart*]—was expressed henceforth in the German words *Anwesen* [presencing] or *Anwesenheit* [presence] and, accordingly, being was expressed in the word *Anwesende* [that which is present or presencing]. At the same time for him there was a movement combined with this meaning of *Anwesen* as a temporal occurrence.

Nevertheless Heidegger did not fail to recognize the different ways in which presence showed itself in the traditional concepts of Being and reality. A different meaning of "moved presence" [*bewegter Gegenwart*] lay in each of the following: Aristotle's "energetic activity" of *ousia*, Scholasticism's *actualitas*, Leibniz' monad, German Idealism's "concept," and Nietzsche's "will to power." Heidegger was convinced that in this transformation presencing as present [*Anwesen als Gegenwart*] became "more and more congealed."

Against this view it might indeed be asked whether or not an increasing dynamization of Being must be seen precisely in the development of modern philosophy, i.e., in the passage from Fichte's act [*Tathandlung*], to Schelling's concept of willing as primal Being [*Ursein*], to Hegel's thought of process, to Nietzsche's concept of the will. In any case, for Heidegger today under the dominance of technology—in which, according to him, that which is real has the character of Being of a "disposable stock" [*bestellbaren Bestandes*]—the present, which is thought of within this Being, has congealed into mere "permanence" [*Beständigkeit*].

One must understand that in order to loosen up this congealing of the temporal character of Being, in order to loosen up this congealed presencing and to recover for it its character as an occurrence, Heidegger attempted to think of presencing in terms of a concept of time entirely different from and opposed to the traditional concept.

This was the object of his last great lecture, "Time and Being," which accomplished the reversal that *Being and Time* was unable to accomplish because thinking was then not sufficiently transformed to be able to do so. This cannot be discussed in detail now, however. In any case, an aim of the late Heidegger was to show that Being, presencing, is an occurrence—the occurrence of the temporalizing [*Zeitigung*] of a time that is to be thought of in an entirely different way.

Since we are asking now about the relation of thinking to this matter, we must remember that for the early Heidegger this new way of thinking was determined by the character of *aletheia*. How is this occurrence of presencing, which is thought of here in terms of time, related to the matter at stake in *aletheia*?

We cannot answer this question without having made clear Heidegger's understanding of the matter underlying *aletheia* as an occurrence of truth. In this lies perhaps his most important contribution to the history of Western thought.

In *Being and Time* the "most original phenomenon of truth" lay in the fact that *Dasein is* essentially its "disclosedness"; that as disclosed it is "in truth"; at the same time, however, it "is in untruth" because as essentially falling [*verfallend*] the closing off and covering over [*Verschlossenheit und Verdeckheit*] belong to its facticity.

In "On the Essence of Truth," in a step that led beyond the analytic of *Dasein* as such, Heidegger proceeded to make visible the phenomenal evidence for an open relational realm [*offenen Bezugsbereich*], without which an object that is standing over against representational thought, which is open for it, cannot reach that representational thought; however, this open relational realm is not created by representational thought; rather it takes it over and presupposes the relational realm. Heidegger later attempted to elucidate this realm by using the term "*Lichtung*" to designate it. Whereas in *Being and Time Lichtung* designated the "Being-illuminated" [*Erleuchtetsein*] of the "There" [*Da*] (which understands Being) of *Dasein* "in itself" (cp. SZ 133 : BT 171), in the "Letter on Humanism" this *Lichtung* of the "There" became that of Being itself, into which man, who understands Being, stands forth, ek-sists (PLW 77 : BW 204 ff.). *Lichtung* is henceforth thought of as an occurrence, an "opening clearing" [*öffendes Lichten*], just as much as the "result of this occurrence" is thought of as the "open region of the clearing" [*das Offene der Lichtung*]. The image with which we can make both clear to ourselves is that of opening a free place in the thicket of the forest. In any case, one sees that for Heidegger after *Being and Time* "*Lichten*" does not mean *"erleuchten"* [illumination]; *"Lichtung"* does not mean *"Licht"* [light]. Rather a ray of light pointed out the fact that there is in general an open region in a clearing that it can cross. Every kind of thought as well as the identity of Being and thought, which defines traditional thought, presupposes that there is the open region of the clearing; and truth can only be what it was traditionally thought to be—namely, evidence, certainty, or correctness of assertions—in the element of and thanks to the open region of the clearing. For this reason, in his last publication Heidegger no longer called this "condition of the possibility" of traditional truth "truth." Above all, however, there can be presence, Being, only because there is the open region and free dimension of the clearing, and *that which* is presencing, beings, can be only for the letting-be [*das Seinlassen*] of man insofar as they stand forth in this open region. Nevertheless—and this is Heidegger's decisive view—Western thinking has hitherto thought of neither the clearing nor the occurrence of presencing of that which is present in that clearing. To think it becomes in a *special* sense the matter and the task of thinking. No longer does the task lie, as it did in the beginning of the Heideggerian path of thinking, in his new determination of "Being and time"; rather, as he wrote in his last essay—which we regard as Heidegger's testament—the title of the task of thinking now reads "clearing and presence" (ZSD 80 : BW 392). Thus, as we have already said, it belongs to this task to think the occurrence of presencing in terms of another kind of time.

Perhaps Heidegger's most important insight lies in seeing that the clearing of the presence of that which is present is in itself simultaneously concealing, indeed concealing the whole of beings. Precisely because we deal with individual beings in their everyday comportment, the whole conceals itself simultaneously concealing, indeed a concealing of the epistemology, but rather as a concealment that is simply intrinsic to the human letting-be of beings. For Heidegger there is a self-concealing that fundamentally withdraws from human uncovering; it is a dimension—which in the essay on truth he called the "mystery" [*das Geheimnis*] (WdW 19 : BW 137)—that denies itself to human uncovering. The self-concealing of this dimension is at the same time—as Heidegger will later indicate and designate as the task of future thinking—a conserving and a sheltering because of and from within which is granted the unconcealment of that which is that prevails at any given time.

This unconcealment of the Being of beings may *not* be represented as if it has left behind its origin [*Herkunft*] out of concealment, out of mystery; rather the unconcealment remains throughout in accord with and thoroughly penetrated by mystery. And precisely for that reason, that which is present as that which is unconcealed also holds itself back in concealment. Therefore, that which is present is also manifest and not manifest [*offenbar und nicht offenbar*].

Although for Heidegger it belongs precisely to the calling of man to remain mindful of this mysterious character of Being and to watch over [*hüten*] the mystery, man nevertheless constantly turns away from it, not out of negligence but on the contrary because forgetting the mystery, this "errancy" [*Irre*], belongs to the "inner constitution of *Dasein*."

At this point, I would like to interrupt my presentation

once more in order to make clear by means of a short recollection with regard to the history of thought wherein I see the significance of this particular Heideggerian concept.

It will be remembered that traditionally from Aristotle to Hegel, which tradition has proved to be the decisive historical influence on us, beings have been considered fundamentally intelligible. For Aristotle this view results from the assumption of the unconditional rule of the principle of complete transparency, of *nous*, of mind. Only because for him, from the perspective of a highest being—whose reality lies in the intellectual comprehension [*geistigen Erfassen*] of itself—the essence of the being (*ousia*, substance) was from the outset based upon the possibility of the intuitive-intellectual contemplation and discursive-logical thought of man did Aristotle grant to man the potential power [*Vermögen*] to see through the essence completely and totally. Later the philosophy of subjectivity, from the "conditions of the possibility of knowledge," attempted to ground rationally the universally valid experiential character that belongs to the objects of experience; and Hegel taught that everything that is is permeated by the absolute concept "in itself" in such a way that thought likewise is able to comprehend it "for itself" and to present it "in and for itself." The philosophy of substantiality, like that of subjectivity, proceeded then from the points that everything that is is illuminable and that the source of this light is the highest being—God. In this sense metaphysics was a "metaphysics of light." Furthermore, it can be said that this metaphysics prevails in a secularized form in the hubris of contemporary confidence in the intelligibility of the universe and belief in the scientific-technical rationalization of society. An entire ensemble of new

40

sciences—from cybernetics to communications research, social technology and biotechnology—serves today for the
steering of such a totally rational society.

Against this historical influence of the fundamental assumption of the tradition that reaches into our own age
Heidegger posed the view that presencing is a coming forth
into unconcealment out of a fundamentally impenetrable
concealment, that is, out of the mystery, and that everything
that has stepped forth remains thoroughly under the sway of
the "mystery." If some future humanity were no longer to
forget this mysterious character of the Being of beings but
rather were to experience it, and if this experience were to
have the force of a radical change of consciousness, then that
humanity would turn away from the belief in the ever-
progressive plannability of the universe.

But now I would like to return to where I interrupted my
presentation. For Heidegger, not only the unconcealment of
the Being of beings—the unconcealment that determines
everything—remains thoroughly attuned [*durchstimmt*] by
concealing, by mystery; for him there also irrevocably prevails within the sphere of the beings already lighted [*gelichte-
ten*: also "cleared"] a concealing in the manner of "dissembling." Heidegger, in "The Origin of the Work of Art,"
says that "if beings would not simulate [*verstellen*] beings,
then we could not be mistaken about them, could not "slip
up"; we could not go astray and go wrong; and, lastly, we
could never misgauge and overreach ourselves" (Hw 42 :
BW 176). That a being as semblance [*Schein*] has the power
to deceive is the condition for our being deceived, "not
conversely," as Heidegger expressly emphasizes. Correspondingly, in his earlier essay, "On the Essence of Truth,"

the "errancy" that belongs to the inner constitution of *Dasein* was also a ground for error, which "extends from the ordinary slipping up, making a mistake and miscalculating, to going astray and venturing too far in one's essential attitudes and decisions" (WdW 22 : BW 136). Later I shall point out one of the important consequences that lies within Heidegger's conception.

In the later Heidegger "errancy" also defines the history of metaphysics. As is well known, he understands history as a sequence of "shapes" [*Gestalten*] in which Being, as the meaning of that which is at any given time, has "sent" itself to metaphysical thought. However, these shapes—these sendings [*Schickungen*]—are at the same time ways of "withdrawal" [*Entzug*] in which that which sends as well as that which has been sent holds itself back. In addition, this holding back, the "*epoché*," withdraws itself by means of forgetfulness in such a way that the experience of the withdrawal as withdrawal is obstructed. In this precise sense metaphysics is for Heidegger a sequence of "epochs of errancy." This sequence is at the same time a heightening, an increasing, of errancy since the errancy that now prevails is total.

In what way is the kind of necessity that lies in this self-escalating sequence considered? It cannot be considered as based on a teleological or Christian eschatological principle because the domination of technology—the end [*das Ende*] of this history—is not for Heidegger a perfection [*Vollendung*]; on the contrary it is a form of perishing, of coming to an end [*Verendungsgestalt*]. Yet these factually diverse forms of "sending" come together in a coherent interrelationship, which Heidegger calls the "history of Being"—and this interrelationship is for him not an arbitrary one. On the other hand, as far as I can see, Heidegger has not clarified the different sort of necessity that governs this relationship, perhaps because, while this history does end in total withdrawal, for him it reaches its end for an entirely different reason. The phenomenon of "clearing," the concealing that belongs to it, and the occurrence of the presencing of that which is present within it—all had manifested themselves in Heidegger's "transformed thinking." It was Heidegger's view that he himself was the first to have had insight into this matter of thinking; that with his thought, since it experienced the withdrawal *as* withdrawal, concealing no longer conceals itself; and that with this the history of Being as the totality of the "epochs of errancy" had reached its end. Such a role is frankly an uncanny one—one that Heidegger was obliged to ascribe to his own thinking.

How did Heidegger define more precisely the occurrence of presencing within the clearing, which is thoroughly permeated by concealing? What fundamental determinations of presencing did he conceive?

Two stations on Heidegger's way to new fundamental determinations of the occurrence of presencing can be distinguished. At first he still conceived of his thinking as made possible by those experiences that in the history of Western thought were already constituted by presencing. In works on thought and language the pre-Socratic philosophers had referred to these experiences through the fundamental words *physis*, *logos*, and *aletheia*. However, they had not really thought the experiences that underlie them. At this station on Heidegger's way, to "think" these experiences became the task of an endeavor to "recollect" [*anzudenken*] that forgotten "first beginning" of our history of thought in order to "think in a preparatory way" [*vorzudenken*] "another beginning" for Western thought.

The usual criticism of Heidegger's late work—namely, that the fundamental determinations unfolded by means of this "recollective preparatory thinking" [*andenkende Vordenken*] are arbitrary—overlooks its legitimation in their character as thinking further those experiences in the first beginning.

A more well-founded critique of course could investigate whether or not the determinations preparatorily thought by Heidegger still can be identified as thinking further this beginning. Furthermore, such a critique could ask: Did Heidegger, at the second station of his way, abandon this legitimating relation back to the first beginning?

This second station on Heidegger's way can be understood only when one recognizes that it is an attempt at utmost concentration upon these fundamental features of presencing. If one proceeds from the fact that in presencing it is obviously a question of the presencing of that which is present, the Being of beings, then one can look away from what is present, beings, and view only presencing, Being for itself. Metaphysics, because of its interest in beings, was prevented from asking about the meaning of Being, the meaning of presencing itself; therefore Heidegger attempts to go the opposite way. He asks only about the fundamental determinations of Being, of presencing itself. Thus his thinking was progressively more determined by a guiding word [*Leitwort*] that he cannot have derived from the early Greeks' experiences of Being. This new word is *Ereignis*. Indeed the word played a role in his earlier writings, but it is in his later publications that it first receives the meaning that makes it possible to think the free dimension of the clearing and, within it and in contrast to metaphysics, to think presencing as a "groundless bringing forth" of that which is present and absent [*An- und Abwesendem*], as a "letting," which as such is precisely not an acting, producing, and rational grounding in the metaphysical sense but rather a groundless uncovering out of concealment. To unfold in its fundamental features the "letting" that is thought here by *Ereignis* now becomes the aim that determines the task of the thinking of the late Heidegger. The words that are to name it ward off all the "rational grounding" thought by metaphysics. I will name a few of these words: *Spielen* [playing], *Schicken* [sending], *geben als lichtend* [giving as clearing]—that is, *verbergendes Reichen einer "Gabe"* [a concealing bestowing of a "gift"] —*ein grundloses Geschehen* [a groundless occurrence], which for Heidegger expresses itself in German in the words *"es gibt"* ["there is," or "it gives"], in connection with which this *"Es"* may not in turn be represented as an underlying grounding substance. Rather it is the giving that withdraws in favor of its gift, which does not give present-at-hand beings but gives that which is not at one's disposal—precisely, the occurrence of presencing. Heidegger named this giving, which sends us on different paths of uncovering, *das "Gewährende"* [the granting]. It is important for the statement of our problem to point out that in the dimension of *Ereignis* this granting constitutes for him the other essence sought by him, which is precisely not "enduring" [*Währen*] in the sense of "remaining."

Heidegger also thought of *Ereignis* here for the first time in the further sense of this guiding word as the giving "letting" of presencing, which allows that which is present and absent in where it belongs, in that it brings everything that is present and absent—always in its way—into that which belongs to it at that moment as its "own" [*Eigenes*], and accordingly, not into the "general" [*Allgemeine*], as is the case in the traditional concept of universal [*Universal*].

Heidegger research has not hitherto occupied itself critically with these fundamental features of the occurrence of presencing, which cannot be legitimated from the interpretation of fundamental words of the early Greeks. It will also not be able to do this as long as it has not worked out a standard that would make it possible at this level—which attempted to push forward into a hitherto unknown dimension—to attain agreement in the sense of a dialogic understanding of a common matter. Any further effort toward the task of developing fundamental features of the occurrence of presencing will for that reason remain exposed to great difficulties.

One final way in which Heidegger attempted to respond [*entsprechen*] to the task of thinking will be only touched on. He anticipated a framework within which future man could dwell in a "more originary" [*ur-sprünglicher*] or—as Heidegger calls it, along with Hölderlin—"poetic" way. This projection rests, on the one hand, on those new fundamental determinations of presencing and, on the other hand, on a concept of the essence of language that Heidegger presumably had gained in his interpretations of Hölderlin's poems. In the element of poetic language the four regions of the world—earth, sky, divinities, mortals—manifest themselves in the specific significations in which Heidegger conceived them in the lecture "The Thing" (VA 163 ff. : PLT 172 ff.). It is the interplay of these significations in which one is mirrored in the other and yet remains a unique individual [*ein eigener*]; it is this groundless occurrence of "world-play" and precisely not a ground that grounds or gives reasons for beings that lets be that which is present. This being that is present, in which those significations of the world-regions come into their own, is the "thing." If man could dwell together with things in the experience of the world's regions in such a way that in his dealings with them they would no longer be encountered only in their serviceability and usefulness, then he would live in the experience of his being mortal and in the experiential knowledge of what it means to be upon the earth and under the sky and both of these in the face of the divine. Heidegger gave the name "poetic dwelling" to this resituated primal form of human *Dasein*. Whether and when such a world, and thereby "poetic dwelling" in it, comes to pass of course can be neither predicted nor calculated in the darkness of the world that prevails at the present time.

From *Ereignen*, as developed here, it can be shown how Heidegger's old question concerning the Being of beings and the difference of both transformed itself fundamentally into the question concerning the relation of "world and thing." One could also ask whether Heidegger did not along with this bring history to a standstill and approach again the traditional idea of a terminal state of history, in which the conditions, by means of which history in general arises and is driven forward, are considered suspended.

But what significance does such thought have in the present situation, which is determined by the domination of technology—a situation in which according to Heidegger Being "is" nothing and nihilism prevails? In the meaning of world and a new "dwelling" of mankind in it, Heidegger believed, could lie the "saving" in the "highest danger" in which man finds himself today. This "highest danger" arises because beings have only the kind of Being of a "disposable stock" and thus there is the danger that man views himself as only a "calculable piece of stock" and completely forgets the role for which he is destined.

The role of man in the occurrence of presencing has purposely not been mentioned before this. Heidegger has often been interpreted as having viewed Being as an independent power that acts upon man, a power that withdraws itself from or manifests [*offenbart*] itself to him—a secularized God, as it were. However, this is a misunderstanding. For Heidegger, from the beginning it was a matter of making visible in a new way the "*belonging*-together" [*Zusammengehören*] of Being and man, as opposed to the metaphysical thought of identity. Without expressly recognizing this as his role in the occurrence of presencing, man always responds by means of his participatory uncovering to the granting which, as the unconcealment that prevails at any given time, sends him upon different paths of uncovering. Today he also responds to the granting, specifically to the "essence" of technology by means of his work, that is, his productive uncovering of beings in the kind of Being of a piece of stock. That man responds to the granting at any given time, that he is able to uncover beings in a responding way—therein lies his ownness [*sein Eigenes*], which is thought here by Heidegger from the guiding word *Ereignis*, because *Ereignis* means, above all, that Being and man are "appropriated" [*zugeeignet*] to one another in the manner of belonging to one another.

That this "character of belonging-to" [*Zugehörigkeit*] announces itself in the essence of technology and exactly how it does so was shown by Heidegger in the lecture "Identity and Difference," which he delivered on the occasion of the five hundredth anniversary of our university. If today man would recognize in this *belonging-to* the role that he plainly has to play in the occurrence of presencing, if he would knowingly "watch over the unconcealment and with it the concealment of every essence upon earth" as though this is already occurring in view of the possibility proper to him of a "poetic dwelling," then this would have fulfilled *one* prerequisite for the overcoming of the domination of technology, for the ascent of the saving. The *other* prerequisite, the unforeseeable beginning of that world-play, would of course have to be added.

We have attempted to present, although in a considerably abridged form, Heidegger's concept of the matter of thinking. Only when one has this matter in view is a fundamental encounter with Heidegger possible. For this encounter one must—as far as the last named station of his way is concerned—keep this in view: Heidegger ventured into a region that had not yet been entered by philosophy at all. By placing himself behind metaphysical thought, he gained the freedom to think in a preparatory way of the fundamental features of a new meaning of Being. If it is once granted that this can be a legitimate task, doubt may set in immediately: Does not such an attempt go beyond that which is possible for philosophizing, indeed beyond the power of human thought? And further: Is there a possibility that the presentation of that which is thought in such an attempt can still claim to be a binding and verifiable presentation? If it is a matter of the fundamental features of Being itself in that which is to be

49

inquired about, then the latter is not a *subjectum* (*hypokeime-non*) to which, as if to some underlying thing, determinations or predicates could be added. However, the elementary grammatical form of our language is the sentence, and it has a subject-predicate structure.

Hegel had also faced the difficulty of having to present by means of the predicative judgment insights of his thought that do not correspond to the grammatical form of the sentence. For that reason he had spoken, especially in the *Science of Logic*, in the form of the "speculative sentence." On the other hand, the reader of Hegel's *Science of Logic* knows *how* its propositions make the grammatical form of the sentence serve in a speculative way. Consequently, he can trace completely the transformation of the sentential form, identify that which is presented, and verify its accordance. In a way similar to that of Hegel, Heidegger insists that what is said by him may not be heard as a mere sentence. We recall his remark that the answer to the question, in case it should be granted someday, would not lie "in an assertion about a state of affairs." On the other hand, he speaks again and again of the "binding force and rigor" of what is thought through transformed thinking, and in his last publication he indicated that they result from the "belonging together" of thinking and presencing within the clearing (ZSD 75 : OTB 68, BW 387). However, how can it ever be determined whether or not a thinking upon that which addressed itself to that thinking in the clearing heard it in an appropriate way and responded to it correctly? This remains the question that troubles us about the binding force of this thinking.

Finally, we ask, In what way did Heidegger meet [*ent-sprochen*] the "task of philosophy" as we characterized it?

He met the task in the way that he thought the occurrence of presencing not with regard to and from beings, but succeeded in thinking another essence of essence: the groundless granting that within the free dimension of the clearing lets unconcealment come forth out of concealment at any given time. This definition of essence takes into account our historical consciousness because it makes thinkable the advent of an entirely different form of reality. Heidegger thus at the same time has also met the further requirement of granting to man a role in this occurring of essence in such a way that his uncovering—be it by means of thinking, poetizing, or acting—remains determined by ''granting,'' by essence conceived in such a way that no danger exists of a historicizing, relativizing, or ''anthropomorphizing'' of this ''essence.'' Moreover, this disclosing, like the traditional definition of identity, is no longer bound to a completed system of determinations of thinking and thoughts since the *''belonging-*together'' of man and Being—a belonging together in which man finds his essence as one who listens and responds—takes the place of this identity.

We have already referred to the possibility of an effect transforming the consciousness of man, an effect that Heidegger's concept of the mysterious character of the unconcealment of Being might have. It is indeed a fact that the aggressive self-confidence of Western man has led to the consequence that he no longer sees the limits of knowledge and that he has lost all awe before that which is in principle closed to him. He is convinced theoretically as well as practically of the progress toward enlightenment of his condition and thereby of the progress toward mastery of it. It seems to me that the present movements that point to the limits of human rationality and planning do not begin from a fundamental-enough point; in their conceptual presuppositions they remain dependent upon that which is negated by them. Herein they could learn from Heidegger. From his insight into that which "*is* today around the globe" (ZSD 2 : OTB 2), from his insight into the character of Being that now rules over us, and from his insight that man must respond to the meaning of presencing that prevails at any given time— from these insights it followed for him that one neither can nor ought to wish away the domination of technology. We must go through the technological age. But under its domination we ought to learn to see how presencing occurs and, from this insight, free ourselves for the hope that someday the world and thing in the significations mentioned above will suddenly arrive for a mankind that is open to them. I believe that this is not a form of anti-enlightenment; it is also not a form of irrationalism, because Heidegger's view after all is based upon presuppositions of thinking that lie beyond rationalism and its antithesis. One may well, I believe, speak of utopianism, but not in a political sense.

At this point, however, the question of whether or not Heidegger thought of a standard,—that is, whether he thought of rules of play for thinking, poetizing, and acting—may not be dismissed. I see the truly critical consequence of thinking about *aletheia* in that for Heidegger concealing in the manner of "dissembling" is the condition for the fact that we can be deceived and "not conversely," and that correspondingly "errancy" also belongs to the inner constitution of human *Dasein* insofar as it can lead him astray in such a way that man "in his essential attitudes and decisions ventures too far." One must then ask, Does not the consequence of this view of Heidegger from his middle period, which he by no means later qualified, lie in the "justification" of factual erring? The unconcealment of presencing that comes forth at any given time, which at that time Heidegger also called the "truth of Being," has for him precisely—as he showed especially in the "Letter on Humanism" (PLW 104 ff. : BW 231 ff.), in which he commented briefly on traditional ethics—the character of an "'appeal" [*Anspruch*]. But does this appeal have the value of a standard in the light of which one who hears the appeal could decide whether in a definite situation he hears correctly or incorrectly, acts well or badly? If there is no such standard for human hearing and responding, then one can never state for any poetizing, thinking, or acting of man whether and to what extent it was deceived by the "dissembling" that unfailingly holds sway throughout the clearing, and whether and to what extent it has been led astray by the errancy that irrevocably holds sway in human *Dasein*. No one could be declared guilty of factual error insofar as he only heard an appeal that addressed itself to him and reponded to it. With this concept, however, all traditional ideas of responsibility, guilt, and conscience—in general all that is handed down to us as ethics and morality from our Judaeo-Christian tradition—would be shaken.

To see this possible consequence clearly does not mean to dismiss Heidegger's entire view. In philosophy there are no such simple decisions concerning rightness and wrongness. Without engaging in his different way of thinking and its matter, without encountering Heidegger on his own ground, one cannot oppose this project. Nor does one experience the great significance that lay in his bold and hazardous attempt to step back behind metaphysics, to think of Being as an occurrence itself, to unfold it in its fundamental determinations and from that to develop the framework for a more originary dwelling and build a new way of Being for man. I felt it was my responsibility to bring this before you and I have attempted to fulfill this responsibility in this first lecture dedicated to the memory of Martin Heidegger.

# Being, Spirit, God

*by Hans-Georg Gadamer*

Whoever has been affected by the thought of Martin Heidegger can no longer read the fundamental words of metaphysics—which are contained in the title of my contribution—as they are read in the tradition of metaphysics. In accordance with the Greeks and Hegel one might find that Being is spirit, and the New Testament tells us that God is spirit; in this way Western tradition formed a meaningful whole that stands by itself. And yet this older way of thinking has seen itself challenged and placed in question ever since modern science, through its methodical asceticism and its critical standards, posited a new concept of knowledge. Philosophical thought cannot ignore its existence, and yet it cannot really integrate it. Philosophy is no longer itself the whole of our knowledge; nor is it a knowing whole. Thus today, after the cock-crowing of positivism, metaphysics in general may seem untrustworthy to many, who are inclined with Nietzsche to consider "Hegel and the other *Schleiermachers*" as mere delayers of what Nietzsche called European nihilism. That this metaphysics, which seemed to have come to a conclusion in its own questioning, would once again gain a head of steam in such a way as to persist as a value-assertive corrective in opposition to modern thought could not be anticipated. Like the great series of concept-molders and system-creators since the seventeenth century, the twentieth century revivalists in their way tried to reconcile modern science with the old metaphysics. That metaphysics itself would once again come into question, that its question—about Being, about the two-thousand-year-old answer that has devolved from it—could once again be asked as if it had never been asked, was not foreseen.

As the young Heidegger began to exercise his first fascination, as unusual sounds rang out from the academic chair—sounds that reminded one of Kierkegaard, Schopenhauer, Nietzsche, and all the other critics of academic philosophy [*Kathederphilosophie*]—even later, as *Being and Time* appeared (wherein, after all, this entire orchestration was placed with full force in the service of the reawakening of the question of Being), one associated him more with these critics of traditional thoughts than with the tradition itself.

This is not surprising, however, since the young Heidegger himself raised the destruction of metaphysics to the status of a password and cautioned his own students against putting him within the series of the "great philosophers." "I am a Christian theologian," he wrote to Karl Löwith in the year 1921.

It could be shown, of course, that it was Christianity that challenged this man's thinking and kept it on the move, that it was ancient transcendence and not modern secularity that he expressed. He was, however, a Christian theologian who, concerning what it means to believe, to be able to become righteous, wished to know more than modern theology offered him. But why, compared with so many who were driven by the same desire and as modern men were not able to

56

abandon the basis of science, was he not actually a theologian but, rather, a thinker? Because he was one who thought. Because it was thinking that was at work in him. Because the passion of thinking made him tremble—as much through the power that this passion exercised·over him as through the boldness of questioning to which it compelled him.

He was not a Christian theologian: he felt no authority to talk of God. But what was necessary in order to talk of God—and that it was not possible to talk about him in the manner in which science talks about its objects—was the question that drove him and pointed to the path of thinking.

Thinking is reflecting about what one knows. It is the moving hither and thither of thoughts, the becoming moved hither and thither by thoughts, possibilities, offers [*Angeboten*], doubts, and new questions. There were in particular two subjects about which Heidegger had to think from early on, inasmuch as he was not able simply to accept them but could not refuse them—Aristotle and Hegel. From the beginning Heidegger informed us of the significance of Aristotle in pointing out the path of his thinking; but Aristotle never articulated clearly the manifold meaning of being [*Seienden*], which he had originated. The conclusion of Heidegger's Duns Scotus book gives evidence of the challenge that Hegel's philosophy presented for him; he called it the most powerful "system of a historical world-view" (DS 241). Hegel marked for Heidegger the breadth of tension between Being and spirit in which, speaking as the young Heidegger did, "the living comprehension of the absolute spirit of God" (DS 238) was established in the age of metaphysics. The book was concerned with surveying this span, not in order to seek the answer to the proper question but to consider what would have to be asked about so that this question was not again misunderstood and an incorrect will-to-know pursued. It was a questioning behind [*Hinterfragen*] the question concerning Being—which metaphysics had asked, and its answer had been to conceive Being as essence and spirit—and, like any question of reflection, Heidegger's question was in search of itself.

The breadth of the tension that it considered in its questioning-behind metaphysics was itself an enigmatic thing—time—not the dimension of our measuring, by means of which we measure when we wish to determine what occurs in our temporal experience as a being, but rather what constitutes Being itself: *Präsenz*, *Anwesenheit*, *Gegenwärtigkeit*. The different meanings of being that Aristotle had distinguished found therein their real ground, and it was thanks to their exhibition that Heidegger's Aristotelian interpretations acquired their proper evidence, by means of which Aristotle pulled one literally to the body. They were genuine philosophical inquiries since they strengthened Aristotle's position vis à vis the entire metaphysical tradition and above all resisted its dissipation in the subjective thought of modern times. That which is truly underlying, which is permanently present of "substance," which maintains itself in the Being of *Entelechie*, which shows itself to be "true"—all of these articulate the strength of this Aristotelian answer, which thinks Being as presence. But Hegel's concept in its grand striving to think Being as spirit and not as object, whose objectivity is comprehended or constituted by the subjectivity of consciousness, was also like an offer: the historicity of spirit and its falling into time, this going astray [*Beirren*] of a self-reflecting historical consciousness, seemed in the presence [*Gegenwärtigkeit*] of the self-knowing spirit to rise above and unite in itself all particularity of the subjective consciousness. As the last Greek, Hegel thinks the question concerning Being within the horizon of time as all encompassing presence. The *logos* of Being—about which the Greeks had asked—and reason in history—about which Hegel had asked—formed the two great hemispheres of this spiritual whole.

We would underestimate the task that Heidegger had set himself—that of overcoming metaphysics—if we did not first see how such questioning based upon the temporal character of Being elevated metaphysics out of the subjective thought of modern times to its full strength and to a new presence [*Gegenwärtigkeit*]. There was the *analogia entis* [analogy of being], which did not permit a universal concept of Being; but there was also the analogy of the good and the Aristotelian critique of the Platonic idea of the good, in which the universal of the concept found its essential limit. They were from early on chief witnesses of the genuinely Heideggerian attempt at thinking. And, finally, the ontologically leading position of "true-Being" [*Wahr-Seins*] (ὄν ὡς ἀληθής), of *nous*, which Heidegger obtained from the last chapter of *Metaphysics*⊖, made Being visible as the presence of that which is presencing as essence. This no longer affords self-consciousness and its immanent reflection [*Reflexion*] the primacy that it had since Descartes, and it restores to thinking the ontological dimension that it had lost in the philosophy of consciousness of modern times.

Hegel's concept of spirit likewise recovers its substance in light of the renewed posing of the question of Being. The concept passes through, as it were, an "enspiritualization."

Spirit, in that it is dialectically unfolded on the way to itself, is thought again in an original way as *pneuma*, as the breath of life, which blows throughout everything extended and divided, or, as Hegel put it, the breath of life, which as the universal blood supports and maintains in itself the circulation of life. This universal concept of life is at the peak of modernity, which means it is thought with regard to self-consciousness, but at the same time it implies a definite transgression of the formal idealism of self-consciousness. The common sphere that holds sway between individuals, the spirit that unites them, is love: I am the you, you are the I, and you and I are the we. From there Hegel found access not only to the existence of a social reality that was more than subjective (in that he understood the latter as objective spirit—a concept that up to the present day governs the social sciences, in which interpretation always governs) but also to a genuine concept of truth which, beyond all conditionality, comes to light as the absolute in art and religion just as in philosophy. The Greek concept of *nous*, reason and spirit, remains the final word of Hegel's System of Science. It is for him the truth of Being, essence (that is, presence), and concept (that is, to be the self-establishing selfhood of that which is presencing).

The force of this metaphysical answer, which extends from Aristotle to Hegel, is stronger than the simplistic appeal that is usually made to the so-called "overcoming of metaphysics" by Heidegger. Heidegger always resisted against being understood as if he had overcome and disposed of metaphysics in this sense. If his question questions behind the question of Being of metaphysics and makes known the horizon of time within which Being can be thought, it nevertheless recognizes in metaphysics a first response, a meeting of the challenge that Being presents. Its answer concerns beings as a whole. The question that burst forth in Heidegger's attempt at thinking also allows this answer of metaphysics to speak anew.

Heidegger himself saw in *Being and Time* only a first preparation for the question of Being. However, in his work something else forced itself to the foreground: his critique of transcendental phenomenology's concept of consciousness. It fit into the contemporary critique of idealism, which was prepared by Karl Barth, Friedrich Gogarten, Friedrich Ebner, and Martin Buber and took place as a resumption of the Kierkegaardian critique of Hegel's absolute idealism. "The essence of *Dasein* lies in its existence" was understood as the priority of *existentia* over *essentia*, and out of such an idealistic misunderstanding of the concept of "essence" arose Sartre's existentialism, an intermediate creation from the speculative themes in Fichte, Hegel, Kierkegaard, Husserl, and Heidegger, which were united in Sartre into a new moral-philosophical and sociocritical force. On the other hand, Oscar Becker sought to minimize *Being and Time* as a further concretizing of the fundamental transcendental-idealistic attitude of Husserl's *Ideen*. The Heideggerian paradox of a hermeneutic of facticity is not, however, an interpretation that claims to "understand" the facticity as such; this would be to wish to understand a real contradiction, the Nothing-as-factual, which is closed off to all "meaning." Rather, a "hermeneutic of facticity" means that existence itself is thought of as the taking place of understanding and interpretation, and therein possesses its ontological distinction. This was incorporated by O. Becker into the trans-

cendental-philosophical concept of Husserl's phenomenological program and reduced to a hermeneutic phenomenology. However, even if one took seriously Heidegger's demand to conceive of the existential [*existentiale*] analytic of
*Dasein* as fundamental ontology, the entire analytic might
still be understood within the horizon of metaphysics. It
could then present nothing [*nichts*] as a kind of counterpart to
classical metaphysics or as a modification of the latter, a
finite metaphysics that would be grounded upon the existen-
tiel [*existentielle*] radicalization of historicity. In fact,
Heidegger himself in his Kant book of 1929 attempted in this
way to integrate into his own questioning the critical factor in
Kant that led Kant to deny Fichte's modification of his work.

This had to appear then as a rejection of classical
metaphysics, because it is indeed grounded upon the infinity
of the intellect, *nous*, or spirit, in which the truth of Being
presents itself as essence and with which everything that is is
associated in its Being-meaning [*Seins-Sinn*]. Here, so it
seems, the eternal was grounded upon the temporal, truth
upon historicity, and with it the secularization of the Christian heritage—which can be seen in Hegel's dialectical
synthesis of absolute spirit—takes over through the resolve
toward the Nothing [*durch die Entschlossenheit zum Nichts
überholt*]. Individuals began looking around for more positive, less dreary moods of *Dasein* than the dread of death or
revived the surmounting of worldly despair through Christian hope. In both cases they failed to recognize the thinking
that stood behind the entire Heideggerian endeavor. For
Heidegger it was always a matter of the "There" [*Da*] in the
*Dasein* of man, a matter of the distinction of existence [*Existenz*], namely, its being beside itself and set out like no other

living essence [*ausser sich zu sein und ausgesetzt zu sein wie kein anderes lebendes Wesen*]. This character of being set out [*Ausgesetztheit*] meant however—as it is worked out in the "Letter on Humanism" addressed to Jean Beaufret (whom, I am happy to acknowledge, is a member of the audience here)—that man as man stands in the open region [*im Offenen*] in such a way that in the end he is nearer to even the most distant divinity than to his own "nature." In the "Letter on Humanism" Heidegger speaks of the "strange appearance of the living essence" and of "our hardly thinking out the abysmal [*abgründigen*] corporeal kinship with animals."

It was a long history of suffering in philosophical passion in which Heidegger undertook to think this "There"—a history of suffering inasmuch as Heidegger's unusual, original, and bold speculative force of language had to battle against the ever-renewed opposition and often overwhelming resistance of language. He himself characterized it as the danger that accompanies this path, namely, that thinking—and that includes his own attempts at thinking—relapses into the language of metaphysics and the way of thinking prescribed by its conceptual character. But there was more than this. There was language itself, his own language, our language, against which Heidegger had to press, often violently, in order to force from it the statement he sought.

It is certainly correct to say that the language and conceptual character of metaphysics governs all of our thinking. This was the path that Greek thought, which developed metaphysics, had taken: questioning the assertion, the sentence, and the judgment as to their objective content and in the end in the mirror of the defining sentence perceiving the Being of beings, the Being of the that which is [*das Was-*

*Sein*], or essence. One of Heidegger's great insights was that he recognized in this early response of metaphysics the origin of that kind of will to know that has produced Western science, its ideal of objectivity, and the technological world culture grounded upon it. It can also be seen that the group of languages to which the Greek language belongs, out of which European thought has developed, has acted in the manner of a preformation of metaphysics. Because the Greek language distinguishes the subject from its predicate, it was thereby predisposed to think of substance and its accidents; thus European thought, through its primordial linguistic history, was already established in its own fate to develop metaphysics, logic, and, in the end, modern science. The strongest reason for going astray is situated in the essence of language itself. It seems almost unavoidable to think of language, which is always there, in such a way that it makes something present [*sie gegenwärtig macht*] and, likewise, to think of reason in such a way that it perceives that which is present or that which is made present [*das Gegenwärtige oder Vergegenwärtigte vernimmt*] and takes everything together as in itself, whether it occurs in mathematical equations, cogent syllogistic chains, suppressed similes, or aphorisms and words of wisdom.

Thus, it is evident that Heidegger's attempt to elevate to thought the *Ereignis* of the "There"—which first and foremost grants [*gibt*] space for all thinking and speaking—even if it strives to avoid the language of metaphysics, still attempts articulation by means of the concept. He also cannot help speaking again and again of the "essence" of things in contrast to the empirical grasp of the world by the sciences without such a use of the word being misleading with regard to the new verbal emphasis on "presencing," which Heidegger's attempt to think of Being in terms of time has lent to the word. The observation first made by Eugen Fink with regard to Husserl holds true for Heidegger as well, namely, that certain fundamental concepts of thinking often remain unthematic and exist only in their operative use. It remains no less true, therefore, that in the continuation of his thought Heidegger's entire effort served the purpose of resisting the being led astray that follows from an accommodation to the language of metaphysics and of enduring the necessity of language, a position into which he saw himself placed by the question about Being when it is no longer conceived as the Being of beings.

This expressed itself first of all in the renunciation of the transcendental self-apprehension of his fundamental ontology, which he had retained in *Being and Time*. The fundamental structure of the temporality of human *Dasein* might thus still be very capable of embracing every temporal character of beings as the condition of their possibility—the contingent as well as the necessary, the fleeting as well as the eternal. On the other hand, Being, which constitutes *Dasein* itself, the Being of the "There," was not such a transcendental condition of the possibility of *Dasein*. It was itself that which comes to pass when *Dasein* is, or, as Heidegger himself expressed it in its first formulation, "when the first man raised his head." When Heidegger used this idiomatic expression in his early Marburg days, we disputed for weeks whether Heidegger had meant Adam or Thales by this first man   you can see that we were at that time still not very far advanced in our understanding.

European thought, however, hardly placed at his disposal

the conceptual means for escaping transcendental self-apprehension. Heidegger found eloquent metaphors with whose help he wrung a new meaning from the fundamental logical and ontological concepts of metaphysics—those of Being and thinking and identity as well as difference. He spoke of the clearing [*Lichtung*], perdurance [*Austrag*], and *Ereignis*, and he sought to once again recognize that which shone through the earliest testimony of Greek thought, which we associate with the names of Anaximander, Parmenides, and Heraclitus. The first steps upon the path to classical metaphysics were made by these beginning thinkers [*anfangenden Denker*], who sought to meet the challenge to which their thinking had to respond—the great challenge of the "There."

Something of this is suggested in the Judeo-Christian theological doctrine of the creation, just as the thought shaped by the Old Testament in general—which experienced hearing the voice of God or his silent refusal—made one far more receptive to the "There" (and its darkening) than to the articulated form and what-content [*Was-Gehalt*] of there-being [*Da-Seiendem*]. Thus Schelling's theosophical speculation concerning ground and existence in God constituted a real fascination for Heidegger when he considered how this speculation sought conceptually to grasp the mystery of revelation. Schelling's remarkable gift for obtaining in and proving from human *Dasein* the fundamental concepts of this occurrence in God made existential experiences visible, which pointed out the limits of all "spiritualistic" metaphysics. This was probably also the point on which Heidegger was able to express sympathy for Karl Jaspers' thought, which saw the law of the day limited by passion for the night.

66

Nonetheless, a liberation from metaphysical language and its inherent consequences was gained neither in Schelling's nor in Jaspers' work.

A renewed encounter with Friedrich Hölderlin—whose poetry was already near to Heidegger not only because he was a fellow countryman of the poet, but also because he was a contemporary of the First World War and this was the time in which the late Hölderlin became well known—made the real breakthrough to his own language possible for him. Hölderlin's poetic work was to accompany him henceforth as a constant point of orientation in his search for the proper language. That showed itself not only in his coming forward with interpretations of Hölderlin (1936) after he had recognized his political error, but also in his undertaking (likewise in 1936) to conceive a work of art as a genuine coming-to-pass of truth; he sought to think of it in terms of the field of tension between world and earth. That "earth" was used as a philosophical concept was something almost perplexingly new. To be sure, Heidegger's analysis of the concept of world—which he brought into relief from the structure of Being-in-the-world and clarified on the basis of referential relations—signified a new twist to the concept of world for the philosophical tradition as well. It led from the cosmological problem to its anthropological analogue. Yet it did have its theological and moral-philosophical predecessors. However, that "earth" now became the theme of philosophy—this elevation of a poetically charged word to the position of a central conceptual metaphor—signified a true breakthrough. As counterconcept to "world," "earth" was not a field of reference aligned only with man. That only in the ensemble [*Zusammenspiel*] of earth and world, that is, in the correlation of sheltering and concealing earth and the ascent of "world," could a philosophical concept of the There and of "truth" be obtained—that was a bold twist by means of which new paths opened themselves to thinking. Hölderlin had untied the tongue of Heidegger's thought.

From early on this had been fundamentally what Heidegger had sought. The question of "Being" was what concerned him. One of the points insisted upon by Heidegger the teacher, from the first, was that the Greek concept of *aletheia* (that is, unconcealment, truth) distinguished the Being of beings and that it did not have its place exclusively in human comportment toward beings, in other words, in "judgment." The place of truth is definitely not in judgment. This signified an ontological deepening of the logical and epistemological concept of truth, but beyond that it pointed to an entirely new dimension. This privative concept of *a-letheia*, this taking away by force, which lifts that which is concealed out of darkness into brightness—and which has led as a final consequence to the explanatory character of European science—requires its counterhold if it is truly to approach Being. The self-showing of that which is, that which shows itself as that which it is, includes, whenever it is, a self-withholding and self-restraining. This first gives to beings, which show themselves, the weight of Being. We know from our own experience how fundamentally the There of human *Dasein* is bound up with its finitude. We know it as the experience of darkness in which as thinkers we stand and into which that which we raise into brightness always sinks back again. We know it as the darkness out of which we come and into which we go. But this darkness is for us not only the darkness that is opposed to the world of light. We are dark to ourselves; thus we are dark. This darkness co-constitutes the Being of our *Dasein*.

Earth, moreover, is not only where light rays are not able to penetrate. The darkness that conceals is likewise the sheltering out of which everything breaks forth into brightness, just as the word breaks forth out of silence. What Kierkegaard opposed to the self-transparency of absolute knowledge, namely, existence, and what Schelling distinguished as that which cannot be prepared for in thought [*das Unvordenkliche*], that which lies ahead [*vorausliegt*] of all thinking, belongs to the truth of Being itself. The poetic symbol of this was, for Heidegger, Hölderlin's invocation of the earth.

It was in connection with the question about the origin of a work of art that Heidegger for the first time exhibited the ontologically constitutive function of earth and not merely its privative and limiting one. Here it was obvious that the idealistic interpretation of a work of art was at a loss for its authentic and distinguished way of Being: to be a work is to stand there or to rise up just as a tree or a mountain and still be language. This There of the work, which almost strikes us dumb through its self-situating presence [*Präsenz*], not only communicates something to us, it also sets us entirely outside of ourselves and imposes its own presence [*Gegenwart*] upon us. There is no longer a grasping, measuring, ordering knowledge of an object that stands before us and over which we could make ourselves masters. It is far more a world into which we ourselves are drawn than something we encounter in our world. So the work of art is with special emphasis the *Ereignis* of the There, in which we are set out.

From here two steps that Heidegger's thought had to take

stand out most clearly. If the work of art is not an object as long as it speaks as a work of art and is not displaced into relations foreign to it—for instance, those of trade and commerce—then in the end it must also be realized that even the thing that is ours possesses an original worldliness and thus the center of a genuine Being as long as it is not displaced into the object-world of manufacturing and marketing. Rilke's thing-poems [*Dinggedichte*] tell us something about this. Again, this Being of the thing does not arise in that which an objective approach through measurement and evaluation can establish about it. It is the totality of a living context that has gone into the thing and is presencing in it. We are always a little like an heir to whom it belongs, like the bequest of a relative, be the thing from a strange life or our own.

The extent to which everyone experiences Being-at-home [*das Zuhausesein*] in his world as Being-at-home in such worlds of works and things, however, becomes fully clear in Being-at-home in the word, which is for all who speak the most intimate home. The word is not only a means of information, as which it does function; it is not a mere sign-thing [*Zeichending*] that refers to something else and that one makes into a sign in order to turn it toward something else. As one word or as the unity of discourse it is therein that we ourselves are entirely at home in such a way that our dwelling in the word is not in general realized by us. Nevertheless, there, where it stands by itself and is a work, in the poem and in thought gathered upon itself, it also emerges for us as that which at bottom it always is. It captivates us. Lingering [*verweilen*] in it means letting it be there [*es dasein lassen*] and holding ourselves in the There of Being.

This is a far cry from that which points out its daily course to the present-day *Dasein* of man. Are there not plainly phenomena, which in our world are pushed aside and deprived of all legitimacy, in which the experience of the Being of concealing, uncovering, and sheltering [*Verbergung, Entbergung und Bergung*] identifies itself for this thinking? The world of a work of art is like a world of the past or one that is disappearing and that refuses us admittance, a world that is without a place in our own world. A perishing aesthetic culture, to which we all owe the sharpening of our senses and our spiritual sensitivity, has more the character of a refined reservation than that of belonging to our world, in which we could be at home. Moreover, that things more and more lose their order of Being and life, washed away by the flood of merchandise and being modishly out for that which is the most recent or latest thing, is a fundamental defining feature of the industrial age in which we live, a feature that of necessity grows stronger and stronger. Even language, this most flexible and pliant possession of every speaker, is visibly congealing more and more into stereotypes and stock-phrases and accommodating itself to the general leveling of life. So it might seem as though Heidegger's orientation, by means of which for him the question concerning Being was filled with demonstrable content, was in truth nothing more than a romantic evocation of a disappearing or past world.

Nevertheless, anyone who is acquainted with Heidegger knows that the revolutionary pathos of his thinking was far removed from ascribing to the honorable efforts toward the preservation of that which is vanishing a real significance for the thoughtful penetration of the occurrence of our world. What distinguished his thinking is the radicality and boldness with which he interpreted the dissipation of Western civilization in the universal technological culture of today as our destiny [*Geschick*] and as the logical development of Western metaphysics. This means, however, that in his way of thinking all the pleasant retardations of this immense process of calculation, power [*Könnens*], and production, which we call cultural life, did not count; rather he considered the boldest radicality of planning and projecting as that which is, as the fateful [*geschickliche*] response of our time to the challenge under which man stands. It presents a matter of greater seriousness for man's character of being set out into the world than any other human pursuit. A long time ago Heidegger anticipated what is today only beginning to soak into the general consciousness: humanity, by means of the bold attack of technological power, in which it has established itself, follows an unavoidable challenge under which it is placed. Heidegger calls this challenge—that is, the Being and path of humanity under the sign of technological civilization—the path toward the uttermost oblivion of Being. Just as metaphysics established itself in the Being of beings, in the Being of the what [*Was-Sein*] or essence, and simulated its genuine Being-set-out [*Ausgesetztsein*] into the There, so the technology of today drives the world establishment to its uttermost oblivion of Being and thus is itself that which is.

But then the concealed presence [*Gegenwart*] of forgetting belongs to all forgetfulness. The presence of Being [*Seinsgegenwart*] proceeds, as it were, next to the oblivion of Being, sporadically lighting up in a moment of absorption and transfering lastingly to *Mnemosyne*, the Muse of thinking. This is also true for thought that considers the most extreme oblivion of Being, toward which our present [*Gegenwart*] is

72

driven, the *mittence* of Being itself. Thus Heidegger characterized his own preparatory thinking [*Vorausdenken*] about that which is as, at the same time, the step back that attempts to think again the beginning as beginning [*Anfang als Anfang*]. Preparatory thinking is not planning and calculating, evaluating and managing; on the contrary, it is thinking of that which is and will be. Preparatory thinking is, therefore, thinking back [*Zurückdenken*] to the beginning, from which even the last step proceeds and can be understood as a consequence. Thinking is always thinking of the beginning. If Heidegger interprets the history of philosophical thought as the transformation of Being and the response of thinking to the challenge of Being as though the whole of our philosophical history is nothing more than an increasing forgetfulness of Being, nevertheless, he knew that all great attempts at thinking seek to think the same thing. They are efforts to remain within the beginning, to articulate and give an account of the challenge of Being. So no other history would have to be narrated if one wished to go through the history of the recollection of Being. It is the same history. The recollection of Being is the thinking accompaniment of the forgetfulness of Being. We remain given over to the partnership that unites all attempts to think. Heidegger saw clearly that such a dialogue unites us all. It is precisely for this reason that in his own contribution to this dialogue he posted the markers—more and more decisively—so that we are directed toward the path of the history of Being, which is our destiny, in such a way that he leads us in every way into the open region of the one question.

He did not end the dialogue, whether one may call it a dialogue of metaphysics, philosophy, or thinking. Nor did he even find for himself an answer to his beginning and all-propelling question, How can one talk of God without reducing him to an object of our knowledge? However, he put his question in such a comprehensive way that no God of the philosophers and perhaps also no God of the theologians can be the answer, and in such a way that we also cannot presume to know the answer. The poet Friedrich Hölderlin was considered by Heidegger as his closest partner in the dialogue which thinking is. His lament of abandonment and his appeal to the vanished gods—but also his knowledge "of the divine [which] we welcomed much indeed"—were to him like a pledge that the dialogue of thinking finds its partner even in the approaching world darkness of consummate homelessness and the remoteness of God. We all take part in this dialogue. The dialogue goes on, since only in the dialogue can the language in which we are at home—even in a more and more estranged world—arise and develop further.

# Heidegger and Natural Science

## by *Carl Friedrich von Weizsäcker*

> Science is one way, and in fact a decisive way, in which everything that is presents itself to us.
>
> Therefore we must say that the reality within which the man of today moves and attempts to endure is, with regard to its fundamental features, determined in increasing measure by what one calls Western European science.
>
> If we reflect on this process, it becomes evident that science has developed in the Western sphere of the world and in its historical era a power formerly nowhere met with upon the earth; in view of this, this power will eventually lay over the entire globe (Heidegger, "Science and Reflection" [VA 45: QT 156].

Our century is a century of natural science. In our century natural science seems to reveal itself as the hard core of modern times. If we had to name one philosopher of our century, we would have no choice but to name Martin Heidegger. Heidegger, however, was not a philosopher of natural science. It was neither the point of departure nor the goal of his thought. How does this make sense? The passage by Heidegger quoted above shows how. Heidegger saw the decisive role of science in our time. He suffered under this time, which was his as well as ours. In his younger years this suffering took the form of a demanding critique, and in his later years it took the form of deep concern and thorough thinking about a fate [*Schicksal*].

Natural science has not up to now understood what Heidegger had to say. Conversely, it seems to me that Heidegger was not able to think natural science down to its foundation. To show this two-sided, unfulfilled task and to take it up as a challenge I have gladly accepted in speaking on Heidegger and natural science today. I will proceed in three steps. First, I would like to discuss once more the historical role, under the title of en-framing [*das Ge-stell*], in which the later Heidegger saw both natural science and technology. Next I will address the ontological problem in a passage in which the early Heidegger decides science's way of seeing. Lastly, I will venture a physicist's response to Heidegger.

## 1. The En-framing

I shall review with a brief commentary based on two works by Heidegger that deal thematically with science. The first is the lecture "the Age of the World-Picture" (1938; in *Holzwege*, 1950); the second consists of two lectures that belong together, "The Question Concerning Technology" and "Science and Reflection" (1953; in *Vorträge und Aufsätze*, 1954).

The first of these lectures begins with the following:

> In metaphysics the essence of being is reflected upon and the essence of truth is decided. Metaphysics grounds an era in that it gives to it a specific interpretation of being and, by means of a specific conception of truth, the ground of its essential form [ZW 69 : QT 115].

76

The era of which Heidegger speaks is modern times. Heidegger sees modern times as determined by metaphysics—and thus by a decision about the essence of truth—although this is a modified form of the metaphysics in Greek philosophy. Heidegger enumerates five essential phenomena of modern times: science, machine technology, aesthetics, culture, and de-divination. The lecture is confined to modern science, which, as distinct from the *doctrina* and *scientia* of the Middle Ages and the Greek 'ἐπιστήμη, is essentially research [*Forschung*]. Research in a realm of being, for example, nature, projects beforehand a specific outline of the essence of this being—in this case of natural events. Heidegger wrote in this first lecture that modern physics is mathematical by means of "the projection of that which is to be nature in the future for the sought-after knowledge of nature—the connection of the motion of self-contained spatiotemporal points of mass" (ZW 72 : QT 119). In the later lecture (WB 60–61 : QT 171–172) Heidegger sees the mathematical preprojection carried on through all transformations of modern physics, even down to quantum theory's critique of objects.

What is the aim of the preprojection? As Heidegger says:

> The facts are to . . . be objective. The procedure must therefore represent the changeable in its changing, bring it to a standstill and nevertheless allow the motion to be a motion . . . The constancy of the changing in the necessity of its course is law. Facts first become clear as the facts that they are within the horizon of rule and law. . . Only because modern physics is essentially mathematical can it be experimental [ZW 73–74 : QT 120–121].

This passage provides an insight into the essence of physics, which ran throughout Kant and is related to Einstein's principle that "theory first decides that which is measurable."[1] This preprojection makes it possible for science to become an industry. As Heidegger reminds us:

> The scholar disappears. His place is taken by the researcher, who exists in research enterprises" (ZW 78 : QT 125).
>
> What conception of being and what concept of truth are grounds for science turning into research? . . . Nature, in advance calculation, and history, in historical verification, are, so to speak, placed [*gestellt*] . . . This objectification of being is achieved in representational thought that aims at bringing every being before itself in such a way that the calculating human being can be secure, and that means certain. Science first comes to be research, and only then, when truth is transformed into the certainty of representational thought [ZW 80 : QT 126–127].

It is with the domination of representational thought that there is a world-picture for the first time—hence the title "The Age of the World-Picture":

> World-picture essentially means, therefore, not a picture of the world but rather conceiving the world as picture [ZW 82 : QT 129].

> The fundamental event of the modern age is the conquest of the world as picture. The word "picture" [*Bild*] now means: "the product of representational production" [*das Gebild des vorstellenden Herstellens*] [ZW 87 : QT 134].

---

1. Cp. W. Heisenberg, *Der Teil and das Ganze, Gespräche im Umkreis der Atomphysik*, München 1969, p. 92.

The lecture that was written fifteen years later, "The Question Concerning Technology," enhances the connection to technology indicated in the former lecture. For Heidegger technology is not applied natural science; on the contrary, it is a specific mode of truth or, as he now says, of uncovering [*Entbergen*], which defines natural science itself (FT 20, 21 : QT 12, 13).

> Technology essences [*west*] in the realm where uncovering and unconcealment, where 'αλήθεια, where truth occurs [FT 21 : QT 13].

> The uncovering that holds sway in modern technology is a provoking [*Herausfordern*] that places [*stellt*] the demand on nature to yield energy, which as such can be provoked and accumulated [FT 22 : QT 14].

Heidegger, in the style of his later works, is playing here on the words associated with *Stellen* ["placing" or "putting"].

> That which is thus disposed [*das so Bestellte*] has its own condition [*Stand*]. We call it stock [*Bestand*] [FT 24 : QT 17].

> Who carries out the provocative placing whereby that which is called real is uncovered as stock? Obviously, man . . . But man does not have unconcealment, wherein that which is real shows itself or withdraws at any given time at his command. . . . Only insofar as man for his part is already provoked to provoke natural energies can this disposing uncovering occur [FT 25 : QT 18].

> We now call that provoking demand, which brings man to dispose of that which uncovers itself as stock, the *en-framing* [FT 27 : QT 19]. Modern physics is the herald, still unknown in its origin, of the en-framing [FT 29 : QT 22].

I suppose that anyone listening to my present lecture does not want to explain away his consternaton by means of an easy rejection of the Heideggerian way of speaking. However, it is at least fitting to sketch carefully this really strange language in conventional language. It is a familiar thought today that natural science and technology make nature available to modern man in a mode of representability, that they make nature representable in the form of availability. Technocrats think: We rule because we know; we know in order to rule; knowledge is power. Social critics and conservationists invert these same thoughts: The form of this knowledge is defined by the will to power [*Machtwillen*]; the untrustworthiness of such science is then often asserted, based upon its devastating effects. Both versions follow the same schema but with opposing values. Man appears in both as the one who acts, as the author of events—by means of his knowledge. That true knowledge is useful is presupposed; therefore natural science appears true to the technocrats and questionable to the social critics and conservationists.

Do Heidegger's thoughts belong to either of these two versions? He will never rank among the technocrats. Does he belong in the group called somewhat loosely "social critics and conservationists?" That his subjective feeling in the face of the world of technology was a feeling of alarm, even of hostility, is only too clear. One could refer to a sentence from his lecture on technology: "Thus, where en-framing prevails there is danger in the highest sense" (FT 36 : QT 28). Heidegger continues with the Hölderlin quotation:

> Where, however, danger is, grows
> the saving also.

80

This is not merely a hope for an unknown saviour. To be sure, not only in the *Der Spiegel* interview but also in a discussion circle in my home in Hamburg, unforgettably, he said to me, "Only God can still save us." But the connection of truth, danger, and saving is indissoluble for him. "The essence of technology is, as a *mittence* of uncovering, the danger" (FT 36 : QT 28). "*Mittence*" is used here as history, specifically, as history whose author is not a man who behaves as if he were independent. Uncovering is truth and thus, retranslated conventionally, the sentence reads: "The essence of technology is the danger, because this essence belongs to the history of truth."

In substance something doubly strange is maintained here: epistemologically—the essence of technology is not the application of truth but truth itself; historically—the truth itself is the danger. It is equally the saving.

The granting [*Gewährende*], which sends one way or another into uncovering, is as such the saving [FT 40 : QT 32].

As long as we represent technology as an instrument we remain stuck in the will to master it. We miss the essence of technology [FT 40 : QT 32].

The essence of technology is in a deep sense ambiguous. Such ambiguity points to the mystery of all uncovering, that is, to the mystery of truth [FT 41 : QT 33].

The irresistability of the disposing and the holding back of the saving pass by one another just as the paths of two stars in motion among the heavenly bodies. But it is this—their passing one another by—that is concealed in their nearness [FT 41 : QT 33].

I prefer not to comment further on these passages. In the composition of his late style, as a sign of his isolation, Heidegger is also precise in the saying, the pointing out, and the passing over in silence of that for which he did not have the capacity to say more.

## 2. Ontology, Logic, and Truth

The dialogue between Heidegger and natural science cannot be guided by a few isolated texts of his late period. These texts belong to the last phase of his life's work. The decision that determines the relationship between natural science and Heidegger's thought falls in his early period. It took place before the first sentence of *Being and Time* was written. The immense labor of thought of his early period is just now beginning to become known to the reading public through the publication of his Marburg lectures. In these lectures Heidegger still speaks the language of science and traditional philosophy; in this language he conducts a dialogue between science and traditional philosophy, and it is quite adequately expressed. He lays bare lucidly and in detail the foundations of this thought and the unclarified questions lying within them. The resolution to use a self-styled terminology in his published work, which begins with *Being and Time*, is a consequence of this critical analysis of language, that is, of traditional thought. It is here, however, that the direct dialogue with traditional thought breaks off; from now on to understand Heidegger's expressions one must accommodate himself to his language as well as to his position in thought [*denkerischen Position*]. Natural science, however, will not adopt Heidegger's new diction. For that reason, the Heidegger of the Marburg lectures is its partner, if it is to be a matter of a dialogue and not a mere hinting; only following such a dialogue is a return to the texts that we read at the beginning meaningful.

Up to now, in the *Gesamtausgabe* two volumes of lectures have been published: Volume 21, *Logik*: *Die Frage nach der Wahrheit*, and Volume 24, *Die Grundprobleme der Phäno-menologie*.[3] Here phenomenology means ontology. In these volumes natural science does not become a theme. In order to carry on a dialogue with natural science, permit me, in anticipation of the third part of my lecture, to touch on the relation of natural science to logic and ontology.

Natural science factually develops toward a systematic unity. The multiplicity of disciplines does not stand in the way of this; on the contrary, it contributes to the acceleration of systematic advance, of which it is the consequence. It appears that in all areas that we are able in any way to include in the title "nature" that the same fundamental laws are valid. Physics is the science that formulates these fundamental laws. This development has long been manifest for the area of the inorganic; in recent decades it has made rapid advances in the area of organic life. One can say at the very least that physicalism—that is, the hypothesis that the laws of physics are the only fundamental laws—is heuristically successful and is nowhere refuted. There is, furthermore, no universally recognized line of demarcation that permits the exclusion of man or certain aspects of human existence from subsumption under the concept of nature. Later I shall return

---

3. Martin Heidegger, *Gesamtausgabe*, Frankfurt a. M.: Vittorio Klostermann, 1975.

to this problem, which is quite unresolved in the scientific consciousness of our time.

Physics itself develops toward a systematic unity. The central discipline of this unity today is quantum theory, which acquired its definitive form under the hands of Bohr and Heisenberg about half a century ago—in those years in which Heidegger was delivering the Marburg lectures and writing *Being and Time*. General or abstract quantum theory can be described as a nonclassical probability calculus. The word "nonclassical" as it is used here signifies formally a multiplicity of possible events that is based upon the estimation of probability, which departs from that which one would derive by the use of classical propositional logic (Boolean algebra). One speaks conveniently of "quantum logic." The foundation of this nonclassical logic lies in a deviation from classical ontology that is not worked out by the physicists but only verbally paraphrased. In quantum theory one can define a possible event only with regard to a possible observer. Here, for the first time in modern physics the subject-object relationship becomes thematic.

It is not my task in this lecture to analyze further quantum theory. What has been said is enough to show us that Heidegger's analysis of the foundations of ontology and logic, if it proves to be correct, is of direct significance for the core of all natural science. Naturally Heidegger himself was fully aware of this even before he became acquainted with quantum theory.

The first part of the lecture course, *Die Grundprobleme der Phänomenologie* (Summer 1927), which was delivered shortly after his writing *Being and Time*, discusses fundamental theses of traditional ontology in four chapters:

1. Kant's thesis: "Being is not a real predicate [*kein reales Prädikat*]".
2. The Scholastic-Aristotelian distinction of essence and existence [*Essenz und Existenz*].
3. The Cartesian confrontation of *res extensa* and *res cogitans*.
4. The logical characterization of Being by means of the copula in the predicative statement [*Satz*].

The introduction establishes the problem as well as Heidegger's projection of its resolution. The ontological difference, "that is, the separation of Being and beings" (22), makes precise the question concerning Being:

Being is the genuine and only theme of philosophy [15].

Being is as a priori prior to beings. Even today the meaning of this a priori—that is, the meaning of the "prior"—and its possibility are not clarified. . . . The "prior" is a temporal determination, but one that is not situated in the chronological order of time, which we measure with the clock. . . [27]. We encounter the Being of a being in the understanding of Being. It is understanding that first of all reveals [*aufschliesst*] or, as we say, discloses [*erschliesst*], something such as Being [24].

There is Being only when there is disclosedness, that is, when truth is. . . There is Being only when truth—that is, *Dasein*—exists [25]. Ontology does not allow itself to be grounded purely ontologically. Its own rendering possible [*Ermöglichung*] is referred back to a being, that is, to something ontic—*Dasein* [26].

Ontology has an ontic foundation; [in the words of Aristotle:] The first science, the science of Being, is theology [26].

If temporality constitutes the meaning of the Being of human *Dasein*, but the understanding of Being belongs to the constitution of the Being of *Dasein*, then this understanding of Being must also become possible only on the ground of temporality. . . The horizon from which something like Being in general becomes understandable is time. We interpret Being from time [22].

The first chapter then immediately paves the way for the second in that in Kant's thesis, Being is not a real predicate, he interprets Being as *existentia* and real predicate as a constituent of *essentia*. The ontic—that is to say, the theological—basis of classical ontology is evident in that Kant developed his thesis within the critique of the proofs of God. Kant's explanation of Being as ''position'' suggests a relation of objects to the faculty of knowledge [*Erkenntnisvermögen*], and thus to the ontic ground of ontology in the knowing subject. To this Heidegger joined the phenomenology of intentionality: ''Perception lets that which is present-at-hand be encountered and as such lets it be freely given'' (98). Being as presence-at-hand is a further clarification of the conception of Being.

The second chapter concludes from the theses of the Scholastics from Thomas to Suarez:

> . . . the distinction of *essentia* and *existentia in ente creato* depends upon whether the interpretation of Being in the sense of existence is oriented in general toward actualization [*Verwirklichung*], that is, toward creation and production [138].

> If created being as that which is created is to be possible, then actuality [*Wirklichkeit*] must be able to be added to possibility, that is, both must in reality be distinct [139].

Heidegger traces this pattern of thought back to Greek ontology. For him the "guiding clue for its interpretation" is "the view of production":

> The potter shapes a pitcher out of clay. . . This is produced by looking [*Hinsehen*] at the anticipated form [*Aussehen*] of the thing to be shaped, to be imprinted [*zu bildenden, prägenden*]. This form of the thing, which is anticipated and sighted beforehand, is that which the Greeks mean ontologically by εἶδος, ἰδέα. The figure [*Gebilde*] that is shaped [*gebildet*] according to the original [*Vorbild*] is as such the image [*Ebenbild*] of the original [150].

By chance the Greek view of production does not allow every being to appear as that which is produced. The figure is produced from material that is found beforehand. "Thus in production we hit precisely upon that which is in need of production" (164). However, for just this reason:

> . . . that which is in need of production can in general be understood and discovered only within an understanding of the Being of production [163].

> The concepts of matter and material have their origin in an understanding of Being that orients itself toward production [164].

However, can every being "be conceived as that-which-is-present-at-hand" (169)? Man can least of all. This leads to the modern subject-object distinction.

The third chapter deals with the distinction between person and thing [*Sache*], essentially as it is defined in Kant's practical philosophy:

> Thus the specific kind of Being of the moral person was situated in free action [*Tun*]. Kant once said: "That is intellectual whose concept is an action." . . . The "I" is "I act," and as such it is intellectual [200].

> Those with intelligence, moral persons, are subjects whose Being is an acting [*Handeln*] [200]

Heidegger's critique of Kant, which leads further, begins thus:

> There is present in Kant a peculiar omission insofar as he does not succeed in originarily determining the unity of the theoretical and practical "I" [207].

> Kant speaks of the *Dasein* of the person as if it were the existence [*Dasein*] of a thing . . . There already lies enclosed in the concept of the thing in itself—whether or not it is able to be recognized in its whatness [*Washeit*]—the traditional ontology of Being-present-at-hand [209].

This leads to an exposé of Heidegger's ontology of *Dasein* as Being-in-the-world, which cannot be summarized here.

The fourth chapter begins with the interpretation of the copula in Hobbes, Mill, and Lotze. It is to be regretted that the early Heidegger treated this tradition and Husserl but not the central figure of modern logic, Gottlob Frege. Heidegger's critique of Frege would have become the Rhodes of his leap through the cold fire of logic. Heidegger's special problem in this chapter is the indifference of Being in the sense of the copula compared to its interpretation according to the classical ontological distinctions, as essence or existence, as person or thing [*Sache*]. I leave open whether or not Heidegger's concept is logically tenable. What is essential for us is the concept of truth that he uses for its explanation.

> The primary character of the assertion [*Aussage*] as "pointing-to" [*Aufweisung*] must be retained. Only from this character of "pointing-to" is the predicative structure of the assertion to be defined. Accordingly, predication is primarily an unfolding of that which is given in advance, namely, an unfolding that shows [*ein aufzeigendes Auseinanderlegen*] [298].

As spoken, the assertion is communication. . . In and through communication one *Dasein* comes with another, the one addressed, into the same relation of Being toward that about which the assertion is, that about which the talk is. . . From all this it becomes clear that the assertion does not have a primary function of knowledge, only a secondary one. A being must already be unveiled for an assertion about it to be possible [299].

From this it then follows that the "is" can be indifferent in its meaning because the different mode of Being is already fixed in the primary understanding of beings. . . The indifference of the copula is not a deficiency; rather it characterizes only the secondary character of all asserting" [301].

Heidegger thus establishes a rank and file. The statement of an assertion as a "pointing-to" is primary compared to its parts. The concept is defined as a possible part of the statement, not the statement as a composition of concepts. The disclosedness of beings is primary compared with the assertion. Truth as unconcealment is primary compared with the truth of the statement. Statements are either correct or incorrect, and only by means of this binary structure is logic as science rendered possible; the theory of correct inference presupposes the possibility of incorrect inference. Truth as unconcealment, however, is the precondition of the distinction between correct and incorrect:

*Dasein* exists in the truth, that is, in the unveiledness of itself and the beings toward which it comports itself. Only because it is already existing essentially in the truth can it as such go astray [*irren*] and can there be the covering-up, dissimulation, and closing-off [*Verdeckung, Verstellung und Verschlossenheit*] of beings [308].

89

And the recourse to the ontic basis of ontology: "There is truth, unveiling, and unveiledness only when and so long as *Dasein* exists" (313).

I need not relate how from these decisions Heidegger's path beyond *Being and Time* leads to the late philosophy with profound inner necessity. However, how ought a present-day physicist—a man who actively and with inner agreement passes through the last phase of the path of metaphysics, which was described by the late Heidegger—respond to these decisions? How do truth and beings, danger and saving, comport themselves for him?

### 3. A Physicist's Response

Up to now physicists have not understood what Heidegger had to say to them. Indeed, for that reason I cannot speak in the name of physics but only in my personal capacity as a physicist. But I am also no longer speaking as an interpreter of Heidegger, because I do not believe that he was able to think through deeply enough the reality [*Realität*] of physics. In relation to Heidegger the response also remains a risky undertaking.

It seems to me that Heidegger saw the historical role of natural science more correctly than either its supporters or its critics. He saw that natural science is fatefully determinative for us, because for modern times it is the central, the authentic, form of truth. Complete clarity on this first came to him in the course of his life, notwithstanding that it was the consequence of the decisions of his Marburg philosophy. This may be a contributing reason for the fact that his late phase in academic philosophy is as yet valued less than the earlier. In the earlier period he still shared the traditional error that natural science is a regional science. This view is indeed not only one that is clear at first glance, even one that is a seemingly self-evident scientific and theoretical statement, but it was also (and still is today to some extent) a Maginot Line, the bastion of a defensive strategy against classical physics' projection of reality. This bastion was to protect such positions as vitalism in biology, the attempt of the Dilthey-Rickerts era to establish the human sciences as essentially independent from the natural sciences, Husserl's regional ontologies, and, in radical simplicity, Cartesian dualism. In the early Heidegger are found more or less peripheral agreements with many of these positions that circulated in his academic environment. However, the direction of the thrust of his critique was opposed to all of them from the very beginning.

If the hope of establishing positive sciences such as vitalist biology or an understanding human science continues in the periphery, in the presupposed regionalization of beings, to avoid the diminishing of reality that lay in the classical projection of physics, he nevertheless destroys this hope at its core. All these sciences represent the being that they study as an object, even if the subjective intention of their representatives proposes the opposite; compare the above extract from ''The Age of the World-Picture'' with regard to the science of history. These sciences are forced to this end through their claim to scientificality, that is, certainty. The intersubjectivity of science appears in them de facto, not founded through a common Being-in-the-truth of the scientists; rather the scientists' communication about their common truth has its root in their claim for the objectivity of the research results.

Lying next to the great project of fundamental ontology, the regional ontologies remained for the early Heidegger equally peripheral. Fundamental ontology was still conceived by him as a scientific phenomenological philosophy which, with the ontological core of the Cartesian question, seriously made the distinction of existing beings from present-at-hand beings, of the existential [*Existenzials*] from the categorical. This is also still a strategy of regionalization. Fundamental ontology was now able to appear as that science that does not objectivize. The compromise character of this position is revealed in the fact that the second volume of *Being and Time* was not published as well as in the renunciation of Heidegger's later writings of the claim of being science. Heidegger's late philosophy, which no longer seeks to occupy a place in the province of science, first gained its clear view of science as a unitary form of truth—the central one for modern times.

This great advance, however, is paid for with a serious loss; and it is with good reason that the experience of running aground accompanies Heidegger's later path of thinking over long stretches. As a physicist I attempt to characterize the loss of science this way: it is the loss of the possibility of even asking about the ground of the factical success of science. In the Marburg lectures, Being as presence-at-hand is the ontological projection that renders science possible. It is ontically founded in the constitution of the Being of man as a producing being [*eines herstellenden Wesens*]. This appears a priori; the physicist would say it is known from prescientific experience. The fundamental ontologist searches for a more complete existential determination of man; in this search he has already left the realms of production and presence-at-hand safely behind him. This is a research situation and not an answer. One may hope, should the existential structures be disclosed, to determine in them more accurately the place of production. The late philosophy, however, sees man in a histofy that is interpreted as *mittence* and in which the un-covering of beings in the en-framing is the last, still-recognizable step. How this truth stands in relation to other modes of truth remains concealed for us precisely by means of this *mittence*. The discussion of *das Ereignis*, which is still blocked [*verstellt*] by the en-framing, remains a sibylline strain.

As a physicist I believe that one of the reasons for this veiledness lies in the fact that the path of science has not come to an end. This obliges me to indicate that which is meant by going-to-the-end [*Zu-Ende-Gehen*] of this path. To do this I shall use language immanent to science while tying this to the remarks made in the second part.

Natural science develops simultaneously toward a sys-tematic unity of laws and an unlimited multiplicity of disci-plines. The conceptual form of its fundamental laws has the possibility of this multiplicity as its logical consequence. For example, fundamental laws of a determinate and presumably penultimate degree have the mathematical form of different-ial equations. A differential equation has, in general, end-lessly many solutions; consequently, it characterizes a class of possible functions. The individual disciplines appear then as theories of certain partial classes of the totality of all solutions or certain approaches to solutions of a partial class. To take the path of natural science to the end does not mean to exhaust the abundance of reality that is describable in terms of natural science, because this is impossible; it means to discover ultimate fundamental laws. Axiomatic mathematics shows how little a science is exhausted through the statement of its fundamental laws. The axioms of Euclidean geometry can be listed on a few printed pages; the abundance of geometrical forms and their relations is an inexhaustible wealth. For their part the fundamental laws, should there be such, again are not the ultimate truth of Being. Heidegger has made clear in a passage cited above that the concept of law already presupposes a projection of the kind of Being of beings as, in the sense of Heidegger's terminology, "representable" [*Vorstellbaren*]. What we want to know philosophically is whether or not there are fundamental laws of physics and, if so, what they define. I will assume that they exist so as not to extend the argument. What they define is not a region of beings but a way of understanding beings. How is this way defined?

The hypothesis that I personally follow is connected with Kant: the fundamental laws of physics express only the conditions of the possibility of objectifiable experience. They are not only regulative principles of pure understanding but of positive laws—just as Kant sought them in the *Metaphysical Elements of Natural Science* and in the *Opus Postumum*; by means of the systematic unity of natural science the problem of irreducible special natural laws is abolished. The abstract quantum theory is a general theory of probability. Probability is quantified possibility. Possibility here is a predicate of future events; thus it is a temporal modality. Experience likewise is a temporal concept; experience means to learn from the past for the future. Objectifiable experience is that which underlies logic. Logic implies the distinction between correct and incorrect. Logic, applied to experience, requires that experience be formulated into decidable alternatives, that is, yes-no decisions in the sense of information theory. The hypothesis says, therefore, that the fundamental laws of physics formulate nothing but the logic of objectifiable experience.

So far, the hypothesis, if I am not mistaken, conforms with no deviation to Heidegger's thought. It has, however, three universal characteristics that go beyond his explicit thought. In the first place, it asserts the necessary systematic unity of natural science on a philosophical basis; it directly breaks with the methodical separation of positive science and philosophy insofar as philosophy remains conceptual. In the second place, it would make comprehensible why a regional demarcation of natural science has never been clearly justified. Natural science in the sense projected here is presumably coextensive with conceptual empirical thought in general. The establishment of this thesis, of course, would require a renewed analysis of conceptual thought and thus of the essence of the concept. From this follows a third, still more comprehensive remark. Science thus defined does not stop at man insofar as something can be said conceptually about him. Besides, because of the theory of evolution the continuity of man with nature has become a permanent part of science. In this situation phenomenological knowledge and empirical natural scientific knowledge are not able, as in former phenomenological approaches, to comport themselves toward one another according to the traditional a priori and a posteriori schema. The reflective or phenomenological self-knowledge of the subject can be checked or corrected by means of causal and natural scientific knowledge. I am justifying here only what has been occurring for a long time in today's science against untenable philosophical defensive positions.

The question concerning the ground of the possibility of natural science is thus joined together in the closest way with the question concerning the ground of the possibility of conceptual thought in general. Here today's science permits an explanation of the ontic foundation of ontology through the insertion of man into nature, that is, the insertion of his history into the history of organic life. The order of precedence discussed above in three steps—unconcealment, statement, concept—has an antecedent in animal behavior. Animal behavior has its own correctness and incorrectness. It is based upon the fact that behavior can succeed or not succeed, but is not identical with such success or failure. Correctness of behavior is *adaequatio actionis ad rem*, adaptation to the conditions of the ecological niche. It is not whether or not the behavior succeeds in the particular case that constitutes its correctness or incorrectness but, on the contrary, whether or not it is in principle adapted to the situation. *Adaequatio* here is not the accordance of the image with the original but the adaptedness of key and lock. Such behavior correctly characterized is the antecedent of the general principle. In turn, the resolution of the principle—which corresponds to the unity of action—into general concepts is first a human accomplishment, which is brought about by means of the faculty of representation; it signifies the step from the capacity to act to the ability to accumulate power. Representation is above all not representation of present-at-hand things; it is representation of possible actions. Thus in *Being and Time* Heidegger puts readiness-to-hand before presence-at-hand. The particular case—hence, that which the empirical theory of knowledge considers as the given—is genetically a late stage of knowledge; it is in reality only the specialized concept. Genetically, there first are statements ("fire!"), then concepts ("the fire," "to burn"), and then proper names ("the burning of Moscow"). There are units of action, however, only in an already disclosed environment. This disclosedness exists beforehand and implicitly; it is not represented and has no need of representation. Becoming conscious of it is something other than representational thinking.

Such considerations accomplish in the midst of science the philosophical circle often mentioned by Heidegger. They take advantage of the language of empirical research on behavior in order to describe the preconditions of conceptual empirical thought, its genetic a priori. This language of empirical science factically presupposes the structures of nature, which are explained causally by physics from fundamental laws. These fundamental laws, however, formulate the way that beings can be given to conceptual-empirical thought, and hence also how organic life, man, and his conceptual-empirical thought itself can be so given. Herewith phenomenology remains a methodic a priori—which, nonetheless, can establish no claim of certainty—an a priori of the step into the circle. For one can explain only causally what one somehow has already perceived and to that extent has already understood.

I would like to make the transition to my conclusion by means of a personal remark. The position toward natural science from which this response issues departs fundamentally from that of Heidegger in each phase of his thought. Heidegger could not have been deluded about this in our personal meetings, which were carried on through four decades. He never attempted to dissuade me from my position; he only constrained me, by means of questions that hit the mark, to make it clear to myself. The presentation of a position that would not have come to understand itself without his aid is a thanks that we can offer to a great man. If I purport to see more in a few places than he was able to see, I am aware that without a doubt I have not been able to perceive that which he had a presentiment of, saw, and expressed in other central places.

I am convinced that in his late period he saw correctly the signature of our age in a decisive point. En-framing is the resolution of reality into conceptual acts of representation and the attempt at the restoration of the whole as a sum of interrelated elements. This conceptual restoration of a whole is today called system theory. This is the inevitable world-picture of the world of willing and understanding, which is open as a possible social way of comportment at the latest since the transformation of nature through agriculture, or perhaps earlier, since the hunting culture. This way of thinking is, by means of the same essential features, truth "as making visible structures and as mortal danger." This truth is at the same time untruth, because the parts represented as independent, be they atomic objects or atomic functional units, are themselves products of the concept. They are reality reflected in a mirror unconscious of itself; they are not themselves real. The saving is, in the midst of this world of the graspable, already there ungraspable. Accessible to planning, and therefore a duty, is the seeking and entering of paths in danger. The confidence in security through planning, the so-called pragmatic optimism of planning, is a means of preventing access to the saving truth. The suffering of the late Heidegger from our world was his gift to it. For with that he did not evade that world or that duty.

# Glossary

Only the most important terms that recur throughout the text have been included in this list. It is meant as source for ready reference in reading the lectures. The full meaning and justification of these translations lies in the lectures—what Hegel had to say about prefaces and philosophy applies *mutatis mutandis* to this glossary and the lectures in this book.

*der Anfang*: beginning
    *anfangend*: beginning

> (For Heidegger *Anfang* means more than a mere starting point in time or history; it also has the sense of a beginning that remains with and is determinative of that of which it is the beginning; in other words, it has the sense of the Greek *arche*.)

*das Anwesen*: presencing
    *die Anwesenheit*: presence
    *das Anwesende*: that which is present (or presencing)
    *die Anwesung*: presencing

> (Unless otherwise indicated in the text, when "presence" or variations thereof occur, it is a translation of a form of *Anwesen*.)

*der Bereich*: realm, sphere, region

*das Bergen*: sheltering
    *Entbergen*: uncovering
    *Verbergen*: concealing
    *Verborgenheit*: concealment

*das Denken*: thinking, thought
    *Andenken*: recollection, remembering
    *Nachdenken*: reflection
    *das zu-Denkende*: that which is to be thought, that which is
                for thinking

    *Vordenken*
    *Vorausdenken*     }  preparatory thinking, thought
    *vorbereitendes Denken*

    (At stake in each of the German terms for preparatory thought is the same: it is a thinking that runs ahead and prepares the way for that which is to come after it. However, as the lectures in the present book make clear, this is not a calculating Promethean forethought but rather a thinking that helps to clear the way for that which is to follow. Indeed, by its very existence it helps to bring about that which is to follow.)

*das Ereignis*: (This term has been left untranslated except for the interpretation that is given in the lectures, especially that of Professor Marx. The reason for this is to preserve its character of being "that which is for thinking," "that which is to be thought"—a facile translation of *Ereignis* would have precisely the opposite effect.)

    *eigen*: proper, appropriate
    *eigensten*: ownmost
    *eigentlich*: authentic
    *ereignen*: to appropriate
    *sich ereignen*: to come to pass

*erschliessen*: to disclose
    *die Erschlossenheit*: disclosedness

*das Freie*: free dimension

*die Gegenwart*: presence, present
    *das Gegenwärtige*: that which is present
    *die Gegenwärtigkeit*: presence

*das Geschehen*: occurrence

*gewähren*: to grant
    *das Gewährende*: the granting

*der Grund*: ground, reason, rational ground,
    *grunden*: to ground
    *begründen*: to ground rationally
    *begründend*: rational

      (The sense of reason or rational is lent to *begründen* and *Grund* not only by their dictionary definitions but also, and more importantly, from Heidegger's disclosure of what these terms signify in the history of Western thought; compare especially Professor Marx's lecture.)

*die Herkunft*: origin

*herrschen*: to prevail, rule
    *die Herrschaft*: dominion, dominance, domination, rule
    *beherrschen*: to govern, rule
    *beherrschbar*: masterable

*hüten*: to watch over

*die Irre*: errancy, going astray
    *das Irren*: erring
    *der Irrtum*: error
    *das Beirren*: going or leading astray

*die Kehre*: the turning

*die Lichtung*: lighting, clearing
    *lichten*: light up, clear

*das Nichts*: Nothing

*das Offene*: open region
    *offenbar*: manifest, open

*das Präsenz*: presence

*das Rettende*: the saving
    *erretten*: to save

*die Sache*: matter

*das Sagen*: Saying (of Being and not man)
    *die Zusage*: address

*schicken*: to send
    *die Schickung*: sending
    *das Schicksal*: fate
    *das Geschick*: destiny, mittence
    *geschicklich*: fateful
    *zuschicken*: to send on

*das Sein*: Being
    *Seiende*: being, a being, beings
    *Seiende im Ganzen*: beings as a whole
    *Vorhandensein*: Being-present-at-hand
    *Vorhandene*: that-which-is-present-at-hand
    *Zuhandensein*: Being-ready-to-hand
    *Zuhandene*: that-which-is-ready-to-hand

*die Sprache*: language
    *sprechen*: to speak
    *der Anspruch*: appeal, claim
    *entsprechen*: respond, correspond

*das Stellen*: placing, putting
    *das Ge-Stell*: the en-framing
    *Bestellen*: disposing
    *Herstellen*: producing, production
    *Vorstellen*: representational thought
    *die Vorstellung*: representation

    (The explanation of this group of terms is to be found in the lectures themselves. However, two comments are in order concerning *das Ge-Stell* and *das Vorstellen*: first, *Vorstellen* is translated as "representational thought" because (a) this is the sense it has in these lectures and in Heidegger in general, and (b) because it keeps representation as a form of thought before our eyes; second, *das Ge-Stell* has been translated as "the en-framing" because it is related not only to *Stellen* but also to the formation and continuation of the world-picture, that is, the "world as picture." Man *puts* or *places* the world in a *frame* like a picture by *viewing* it as such and as the *product* of his *representation* of it. On this see especially the first and second sections of Professor Weizsäcker's lecture. It may also be noted that the *activity* of framing or structuring reality like a product is preserved in the term "en-framing.")

*die Unverborgenheit*: unconcealment
*die Ursprung*: origin
    *ursprünglich*: originary, original

*verändern*: to change, alter

*die Vergessenheit*: forgetfulness, oblivion

*das Verhalten*: comportment, behavior

*verschliessen*: to close off
    *die Verschlossenheit*: closing off

*die Wahrheit*: truth

*der Wandel*: transformation
    *sich wandeln*: self-transforming
    *(sich) verwandeln*: to transform

*wahren*: to preserve
    *verwahren*: to conserve

*das Wesen*: essence
    *wesen*: to essence

        (*Wesen* used as a verb signifies that something comes to presence as that which it is, in other words, that something comes to be in the way proper to it. The use of *wesen* as a verb is a further attempt by Heidegger to break free of the traditional distinction of *essentia* and *existentia* and to reintroduce the temporal character of Being.)